BASKETBALL ALL-STARS

STATS • PROFILES • TOP PLAYERS

WELBECK

CHILDREN'S BOOKS

Published in 2024
by Welbeck Children's Books
An imprint of Hachette Children's Group
Text copyright © David Clayton 2024
Design copyright © Hodder & Stoughton Limited

Mortimer Children's Book
An imprint of Hachette Children's Group
Part of Hodder & Stoughton Limited
Carmelite House, 50 Victoria Embankment
London EC4Y 0DZ

An Hachette UK Company
www.hachette.co.uk
www.hachettechildrens.co.uk

DISCLAIMER

Active stats correct as of 01/03/2024

10 9 8 7 6 5 4 3 2 1
ISBN 978 1 8045 3729 9

Printed and bound in Guangdong, China

Author: David Clayton
Senior Commissioning Editor: Suhel Ahmed
Design Manager: Matt Drew
Picture research: Paul Langan
Production: Melanie Robertson

PICTURE CREDITS

The publishers would like to thank the following sources for their kind permission to reproduce the pictures in this book.

GETTY IMAGES: Mansoor Ahmed/WireImage 80; Brian Babineau/NBAE 52; Bill Baptist/NBAE 9BR, 20, 76, 82; David Becker 56; Andrew D. Bernstein/NBAE 66, 75, 81, 85, 97, 105; Adam Bettcher 112TR; Bettmann 69, 99; Vernon Biever/NBAE 12, 48, 92, 93; Lisa Blumenfeld 28; Simon Bruty/Allsport 50; Dylan Buell 17; Nat Butler/NBAE 31; Nathaniel S. Butler/NBAE 10-11, 24, 53, 67, 79, 95; Steph Chambers 26; D. Clarke Evans/NBAE 42; Chris Coduto 88; Ronald Cortes 71; Chris Covatta/NBAE 94; Scott Cunningham/NBAE 90, 96; Jonathan Daniel/Allsport 104; Tim DeFrisco /Allsport 47; Ned Dishman/NBAE 27; Brian Drake/NBAE 5, 91; Mike Ehrmann 107; Garrett W. Ellwood/NBAE 57; Eric Espada 8; Focus on Sport 32, 36, 37, 61, 108; Sam Forencich/NBAE 41; Jesse D. Garrabrant/NBAE 89, 111; Joshua Gateley 112BL; Barry Gossage/NBAE 112BR; Noah Graham/NBAE 6, 19, 29, 73; Adam Hagy/NBAE 112BC; Jeff Haynes/NBAE 39; Andy Hayt/NBAE 21; Thearon W. Henderson 9TL, 34; Tommy Hindley/Professional Sport/Popperfoto 106; Harry How 35, 65; Ignelzi/AFP 51; Glenn James/NBAE 101; George Kalinsky 55; Streeter Lecka 18; Neil Leifer/NBAE 49; Bryan Lynn/Icon Sportswire 102; Ronald Martinez 43; Chris McGrath 62; Jim McIsaac 112TC; Darren McNamara/Allsport 15; Fernando Medina/NBAE 30; Ethan Miller 64; Pedja Milosavljevic/DeFodi Images 16; Paul Natkin 33; Adam Pantozzi/NBAE 70; Joe Patronite/Allsport 40; Christian Petersen 9R, 45, 72, 87, 110; Rich Pilling/NBAE 77; Mike Powell 9TR, 68; Dick Raphael/NBAE 54, 58, 59, 98; Michael Reaves 38, 86; Wen Roberts/NBAE 22, 23, 109; Jim Rogash 14; Dustin Satloff 103; Roberto Schmidt/AFP 63; Gregory Shamus 9BL, 44; Kent Smith/NBAE 112TL; Sporting News 78; Rick Stewart/Allsport 13, 25; Dale Tait/NBAE 100; Noren Trotman/NBAE 83; Jerry Wachter/NBAE 60; Rocky Widner/NBAE 46, 74, 84
OTHER: Pictogram studi/Shutterstock.com, Vecteezy.com

Every effort has been made to acknowledge correctly and contact the source and/or copyright holder of each picture any unintentional errors or omissions will be corrected in future editions of this book.

CONTENTS

INTRODUCTION

Welcome to *Basketball All-Stars* — the exciting book featuring the best players to have ever played the game!

From Elgin Baylor to Kobe Bryant and from Lisa Leslie to Diana Taurasi, we've selected 50 of the best from America's National Basketball Association (NBA) and Women's National Basketball Association (WNBA) - the best two leagues in the world. You'll meet these elite competitors and iconic personalities who have elevated the sport and created history with their skill, athleticism and achievements, bringing joy to millions of fans throughout the world.

Our top picks span the decades since these two elite leagues were formed and cover their most iconic eras up to the present day. This includes the legends from the past such as Wilt Chamberlain and Julius Erving, who revolutionised the game with their technique, explosiveness, and artistry, all the way to the modern-day greats such as LeBron James and Candace Parker, who are taking individual achievements to dizzying heights with their longevity and consistency!

If you're after an objective appraisal of their achievements then look no further! We include the official career stats of all the stars we feature in the book to give you a cool snapshot of their impact on the basketball court. Feel free to compare and contrast the stats of these basketball greats and maybe build a picture of who might make it into your very own all-time Dream Team.

Almost all the players who play in the NBA come through the NBA draft process - an annual event where 60 college players or international basketballers are chosen by professional teams to join their roster. For each player, you'll find out when during the draft process they were picked, which will give you an idea of the promise they showed at junior level before they became a superstar.

Get ready to be amazed by the brilliance of basketball's greatest icons...

NBA legend Michael Jordan was not only a brilliant athlete but he also had an equally brilliant winning mindset.

GUIDE TO THE GAME

A basketball game is made up of two teams of five players and the object for each team is to score points by shooting the ball through a hoop that is elevated 10 feet (9 feet in WNBA) above the ground.

Professional games played in NBA each last a total of 48 minutes, divided into four quarters of 12 minutes. With time-outs, the half-time break and other stoppages, a game can sometimes stretch to up to two-and-a-half hours. Games in the WNBA are slightly shorter with four 10-minute quarters.

To win a game, a team must score more field goals than the other. Field goals are any baskets scored during a game and can be worth two or three points depending on where the shot is taken from. There are various types of field goal, such as slam dunks, tip-ins, layups and jump shots.

POINTS SCORING

1 POINT
Should a team be awarded a technical foul, between one and three shots are awarded and each shot scored is awarded with one point.

2 POINTS
If a shot is scored from inside the three-point line, two points are awarded.

3 POINTS
To score the maximum point score of three, a shot must successfully be scored from outside the three-point line.

WHAT THE STATS MEAN

You will see a stat dial for every star player featured in the book. This offers a snapshot of how effective each player is/was in different aspects of the game throughout their career. You can use the numbers to make comparisons between players and see just how awesome they are/were on the court. Below is a key explaining what the figures mean.

NBA/WNBA MVP
MOST VALUABLE PLAYER
The number of times a player has received the Most Valuable Player award in a competition, league or team.

CAREER POINTS
The total number of points scored over a player's career in the NBA/WNBA averaged over their career.

ALL-STAR GAMES
The number of times a player has been selected for the exhibition game hosted annually by the NBA/WNBA to showcase 24 of the league's star players.

APG
ASSISTS PER GAME
The number of assists per game averaged out over a player's career.

PPG
POINTS PER GAME
The average number of career points scored per game by a player.

CAREER POINTS
38,387

ALL-STAR GAMES
19

NBA MVP
6

APG
3.6

PPG
24.6

ASSISTS
5660

REBOUNDS
17440

RPG
11.2

ASSISTS
This refers to the total number of passes made by the player to a teammate over a career that has led to a field goal.

RPG
REBOUND PER GAME
The average number or rebounds a player scores per game, accumulated and averaged over their career.

REBOUNDS
When the opposition takes a shot and misses, the player of the defence team who retrieves the ball is credited with the rebound. This figure is the total number of rebounds credited to the player over their career.

KEY POSITIONS

A basketball team can have a lot of players, but only five can play in a game at any one time. Players in a basketball game have assigned basketball positions: centre, power forward, small forward, point guard and shooting guard.

POSITIONAL GUIDE

The graphic shows the five basic positions on the basketball court. The positions each perform different roles and require specific skills, which combine to create the ultimate team!

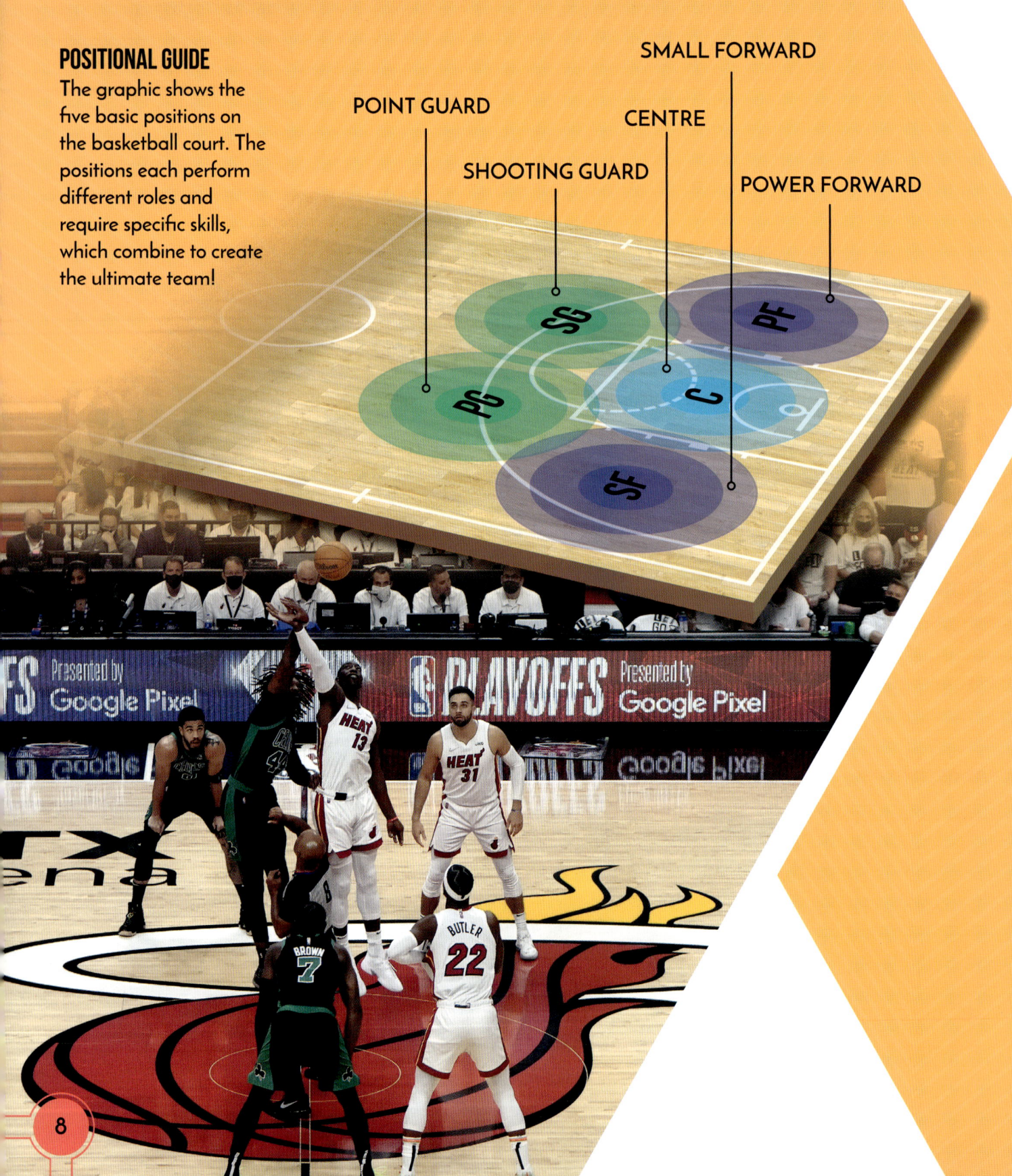

POINT GUARD

SMALL FORWARD

CENTRE

SHOOTING GUARD

POWER FORWARD

SG

PF

PG

C

SF

Stephen Curry

PG
POINT GUARD
Point guards are pivotal to any team – they run the offence and are often the team's best dribbler and passer. They defend against their opponents' point guard, stealing the ball whenever possible and regain possession.

Michael Jordan

SG
SHOOTING GUARD
As per the description, a shooting guard will normally be the team's best shooter who is able to shoot from a distance and dribble well.

ATTACK/DEFENCE
Unlike other sports, all basketball players play both offence and defence and the ability to switch quickly between the two is key to success.

C
CENTRE
A centre is the team's tallest player. Their main focus is offence and therefore play closest to the basket, trying to score shots or putting rebounds in. In defence, they will do the opposite, trying to block shots and stop rebounds.

Lisa Leslie

Kevin Durant

SF
SMALL FORWARD
Small forwards play against smaller and taller players and have license to play all over the court and can score from distance or near the basket.

Charles Barkley

PF
POWER FORWARD
The power forward is similar to the centre, playing near the basket, rebounding, and defending against the taller players. They have the advantage of being able to take longer shots than centres.

STARS OF THE GAME

The NBA in the USA is the best professional basketball league in the world. Founded in 1946 and featuring the nation's top 29 teams, plus Canada's Toronto Raptors, the NBA is where you'll see the game's best skills, teamwork and amazing athleticism all combining to put a dazzling display on court.

The WNBA was set up in 1996 and has since grown to become the home for the world's best women's basketball talent. The league consists of 12 fiercely competitive teams and is committed to empowering female athletes. In the next 100 pages you'll be introduced to 50 of the best-ever players from both leagues. By studying their thrilling stats you'll discover just why they have left an indelible mark on the game.

DID YOU KNOW?
The US Women's Basketball Team has made 11 appearances in the Summer Olympic Games, winning the gold medal a record nine times.

NBA legend LeBron James is perhaps the most versatile player ever. He has played all five positions to a championship-winning level.

NATIONALITY 🇺🇸 USA

33 **40**

TEAMS
Milwaukee Bucks (1969-75),
LA Lakers (1975-89)

POSITION	Centre
ACTIVE YEARS	1969-1989
DATE OF BIRTH	16 April 1947
BIRTHPLACE	Harlem, New York
DRAFT	1969 R1 Pick 1
HEIGHT	218.4 cm (7 ft 2 in)

CAREER POINTS
38,387

APG
3.6

ALL-STAR GAMES
19

PPG
24.6

NBA MVP
6

ASSISTS
5,660

REBOUNDS
17,440

RPG
11.2

ACTIVE AREAS

SG

PF

PG

C

PG

SF

KAREEM ABDUL-JABBAR

An undisputed legend of the sport, Kareem Abdul-Jabbar was born Ferdinand Lewis Alcindor Junior and raised on the tough streets of the Inwood projects in Manhattan. The tall teenager excelled in basketball in high school and college, where his slam-dunking ability was on another level!

BUCKS
33

He was drafted by the Milwaukee Bucks in 1969, and in a career that spanned two decades set the all-time NBA points scoring record in 1984 — a record that lasted 39 years.

TOP 5 NOTABLE HONOURS

- 2x NBA Finals MVP: (1971, 1985)
- 2x NBA Scoring Champion: (1971, 1972)
- 10x All NBA First Team: (1971—1974, 1976, 1977, 1980, 1981, 1984, 1986)
- NBA 35th, 50th and 75th Anniversary Team*
- 1x NBA Rookie of the Year: (1970)

*The NBA has named four teams throughout its history to celebrate a milestone anniversary —25th (1971), 35th (1980), 50th (1996) and 75th (2021). These teams honour its greatest all-time players.

DID YOU KNOW?

Both Milwaukee Bucks and LA Lakers retired Kareem's No.33 shirt after he left each team.

RAY ALLEN

Ray Allen is among the greatest three-point shooters of all time, holding the record for most three-pointers scored from 2011 to 2021. During his peak, he wowed crowds with his all-around offence game — his silky smooth jump shot was particularly eye-catching.

NATIONALITY 🇺🇸 USA

34 **20**

TEAMS
Milwaukee Bucks (1996-2003, Seattle SuperSonics (2003-07), Boston Celtics (2007-12), Miami Heat (2012-14)

POSITION	Shooting Guard
ACTIVE YEARS	1996-2014
DATE OF BIRTH	20 July 1975
BIRTHPLACE	Merced, California
DRAFT	1996 R1 Pick 5
HEIGHT	195.6 cm (6 ft 5 in)

CAREER POINTS
24,505

APG
3.4

PPG
18.9

ALL-STAR GAMES
10

NBA MVP
0

ASSISTS
4,361

REBOUNDS
5,272

RPG
4.1

ACTIVE AREAS

SG PF PG C SF

In the 2013 NBA Finals, Allen is famous for hitting one of the most iconic shots in NBA history. As well as his achievements in the NBA and Olympic Games, he is a Naismith Memorial Hall of Fame inductee.

TOP 5 NOTABLE HONOURS
- 1x Olympic gold medal – Men's Basketball Team: (2000)
- 2× NBA Champion: (2008, 2013)
- NBA 75th Anniversary Team
- 1x NBA Sportsmanship Award: (2003)
- 1x USA Basketball Male Athlete of the Year: (1995)

DID YOU KNOW?
Allen claims he has borderline obsessive-compulsive disorder (OCD) – suggesting that his perfectionist shooting style was the result of practising obsessively.

NATIONALITY Greece

34

TEAMS
Filathlitikos - *Greek league* (2011-13),
Milwaukee Bucks (2013—)

POSITION	Sm. Forward/Pw. Forward
ACTIVE YEARS	2011-present
DATE OF BIRTH	6 December 1994
BIRTHPLACE	Athens, Greece
DRAFT	2013 R1 Pick 15
HEIGHT	213.4 cm (7 ft)

CAREER POINTS
18,252

APG
4.8

PPG
23.3

ALL-STAR GAMES
8

NBA MVP
2

ASSISTS
3,790

REBOUNDS
7,608

RPG
9.7

GIANNIS ANTETOKOUNMPO

Born in Greece to Nigerian parents, Milwaukee Bucks power forward Giannis Antetokounmpo is one of the most decorated players in NBA history, not to mention one of the greatest European players ever.

ACTIVE AREAS

SG

PF

PG

C

SF

ΕΛΛΑΣ

34

ΟΠΑΠ

Nicknamed the 'Greek Freak', his versatility is among his greatest strengths, matched by an athleticism that allows him to operate highly effectively in most positions. Antetokounmpo's style of play and adaptability have led many to believe his style is a blueprint for future stars of the game.

TOP 5 NOTABLE HONOURS
- 1x NBA Champion: (2021)
- 1x NBA Finals MVP: (2021)
- NBA 75th Anniversary Team
- 1x NBA All-Star Game MVP Award: (2021)
- 1x NBA Defensive Player of the Year: (2020)

DID YOU KNOW?
Antetokounmpo was the first non-American to win the NBA All-Star Game MVP Award when he scored 35 points in 2021. His average of 25.1 points is the highest for a player who has played at least two All-Star games.

NATIONALITY 🇺🇸 USA

| 15 | 7 | 00 |

TEAMS Denver Nuggets (2003-11), New York Knicks (2011-17), Oklahoma City Thunder (2017-18), Houston Rockets (2018-19), Portland Trail Blazers (2019-21), LA Lakers (2021-22)

POSITION	Sm. Forward/Pw. Forward
ACTIVE YEARS	2003-2022
DATE OF BIRTH	29 May 1984
BIRTHPLACE	Brooklyn, New York
DRAFT	2003 R1 Pick 3
HEIGHT	200.7 cm (6 ft 7 in)

CARMELO ANTHONY

Sent from Baltimore to West Virginia by his mother, who was concerned her son was going down the wrong path, Anthony excelled in college basketball and went on to become one of NBA's most prolific points scorers. Inside or outside, long- or mid-range, his ability to find the basket was ever-present throughout a 19-year career.

CAREER POINTS
28,289

APG **2.7**

PPG **22.5**

ALL-STAR GAMES **10**

NBA MVP **0**

ASSISTS **3,422**

REBOUNDS **7,808**

RPG **6.2**

ACTIVE AREAS

SG · PF · PG · C · SF

Anthony made the majority of his appearances for the Denver Nuggets and the New York Knicks, and was an absolute powerhouse in his peak years, specifically as a one-on-one scorer.

TOP 5 NOTABLE HONOURS
- 3x Olympic gold medal — Men's Basketball Team: (2008, 2012, 2016)
- 1x NBA Scoring Champion: (2013)
- NBA 75th Anniversary Team
- 2x USA Basketball Male Athlete of the Year: (2006, 2016)
- 1x First-team Parade All-American: (2002)

DID YOU KNOW?
Carmelo Anthony was once saved from drowning by LeBron James during a boating trip in the Bahamas.

TEAMS
Philadelphia 76ers (1984-92), Phoenix Suns (1992-96), Houston Rockets (1996-2000)

POSITION	Sm. Forward/Pw. Forward
ACTIVE YEARS	1984-2000
DATE OF BIRTH	20 February 1963
BIRTHPLACE	Leeds, Alabama
DRAFT	1984 R1 Pick 5
HEIGHT	198.1 cm (6 ft 6 in)

CHARLES BARKLEY

Nicknamed the 'Round Mound of Rebound' because of his stocky build, Charles Barkley is a true NBA giant both in terms of fame and achievements. He was predominantly a power forward but possessed an all-around game capable of hurting the opposition with jump shots outside the arc.

CAREER POINTS
23,757

APG
3.9

PPG
22.1

ALL-STAR GAMES
11

NBA MVP
1

ASSISTS
4,215

REBOUNDS
12,546

RPG
11.7

ACTIVE AREAS

SG

PF

PG

C

SF

He became one of the sport's all-time greats during a golden 16-year career, which saw him become a double Olympic champion for the USA. The only missing honour on his impressive resume is that of NBA champion.

TOP 5 NOTABLE HONOURS

- 2x Olympic gold medal — Men's Basketball Team: (1992, 1996)
- 1x NBA All-Star Game MVP: (1991)
- 4x All-NBA First Team: (1988–1991, 1993)
- 1x NBA Rebounding Leader: (1987)
- NBA 50th and 75th Anniversary Team

DID YOU KNOW?

At 1.98m tall, Charles Barkley is the shortest player in NBA history to lead the league in rebounding (1986–1987)!

NATIONALITY 🇺🇸 USA

34 22

TEAMS
Minneapolis/LA Lakers (1958-71)

POSITION	Small Forward
ACTIVE YEARS	1958-1971
DATE OF BIRTH	16 September 1934
BIRTHPLACE	Washington DC
DRAFT	1958 R1 Pick 1
HEIGHT	195.6 cm (6 ft 5 in)

CAREER POINTS
23,149

APG
4.3

ALL-STAR GAMES
⭐ **11**

PPG
27.4

NBA MVP
0

ASSISTS
3,650

REBOUNDS
11,463

RPG
13.5

ACTIVE AREAS

SG PF PG C SF

ELGIN BAYLOR

The legendary Elgin Baylor excelled at defence, offence and rebounding — where he was considered one of the best. A gifted passer and shooter, he was shorter than many forwards, but possessed the strength to power through defenders or beat them with his natural guile and grace.

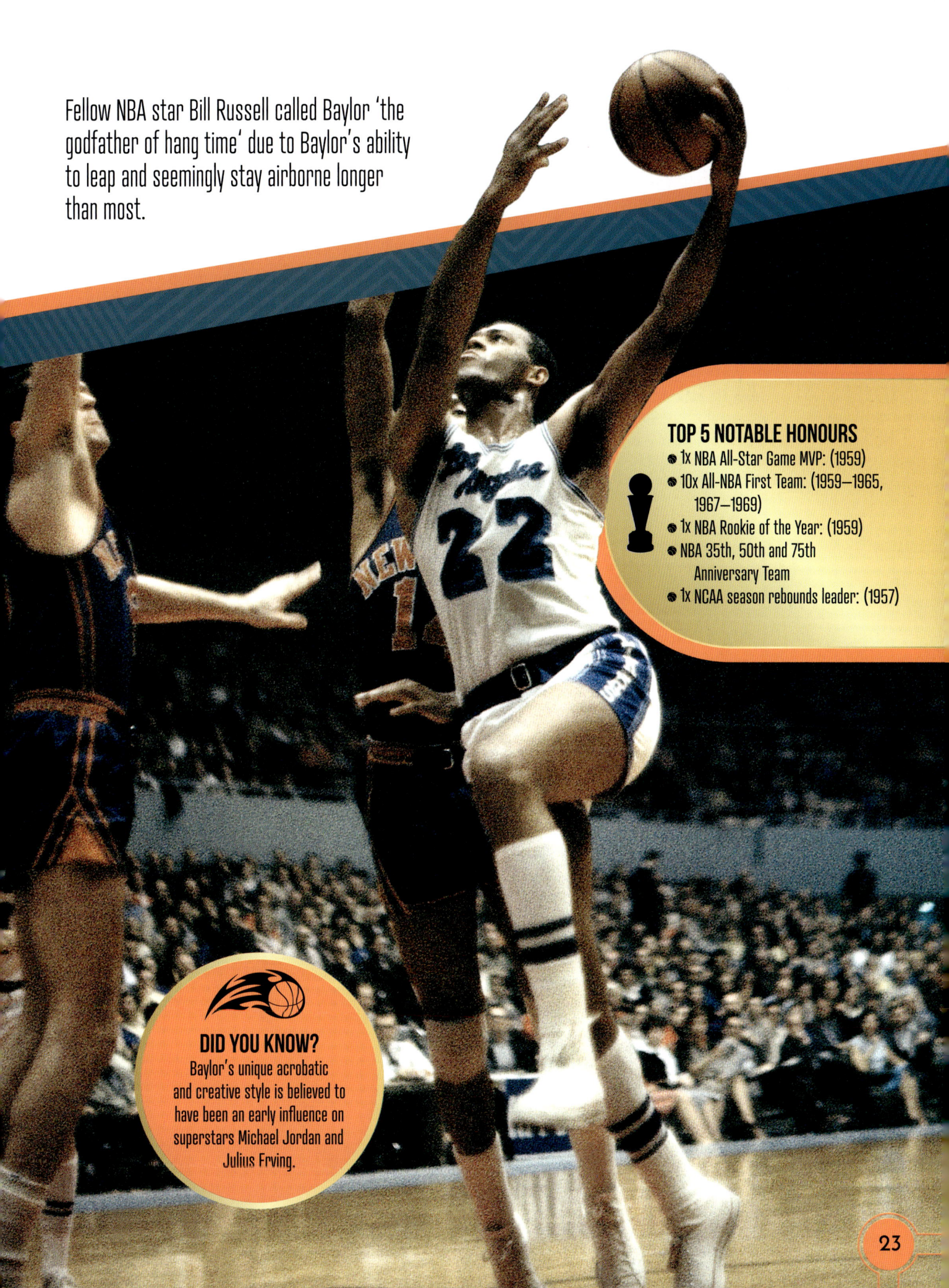

Fellow NBA star Bill Russell called Baylor 'the godfather of hang time' due to Baylor's ability to leap and seemingly stay airborne longer than most.

TOP 5 NOTABLE HONOURS
- 1x NBA All-Star Game MVP: (1959)
- 10x All-NBA First Team: (1959–1965, 1967–1969)
- 1x NBA Rookie of the Year: (1959)
- NBA 35th, 50th and 75th Anniversary Team
- 1x NCAA season rebounds leader: (1957)

DID YOU KNOW?
Baylor's unique acrobatic and creative style is believed to have been an early influence on superstars Michael Jordan and Julius Erving.

NATIONALITY 🇺🇸 USA

33

TEAMS
Boston Celtics (1979-92)

POSITION	Sm. Forward/Pw. Forward
ACTIVE YEARS	1979-1992
DATE OF BIRTH	7 December 1956
BIRTHPLACE	West Baden Springs, Idaho
DRAFT	1978 R1 Pick 6
HEIGHT	205.7 cm (6 ft 9 in)

CAREER POINTS
21,791

APG
6.3

PPG
24.3

ALL-STAR GAMES
12

NBA MVP
3

ASSISTS
5,695

REBOUNDS
8,974

RPG
10.00

ACTIVE AREAS

SG

PF

PG

C

SF

LARRY BIRD

Three-time NBA champion Larry Bird might not be the most athletic in the list of basketball's all-time greats, but he was highly skilled, super competitive and mentally tough. He was also one of the best clutch performers (excelling in high-pressure situations) in the history of the game.

A Boston Celtics legend, he spent his entire career with the team, leaving a legacy that places him in one of the greatest teams in NBA history.

TOP 5 NOTABLE HONOURS
- 3x NBA Champion: (1981, 1984, 1986)
- 2x NBA Finals MVP: (1984, 1986)
- NBA 50th and 75th Anniversary Team
- NBA All-Star Game MVP: (1982)
- NBA Lifetime Achievement Award: (2019)

DID YOU KNOW?
Prior to July 2023, when Twitter was rebranded as 'X', the social networking site's bird logo was named 'Larry' in honour of Larry Bird!

10

TEAMS
Seattle Storm (2002-2022)

POSITION	Point Guard
ACTIVE YEARS	2002-2022
DATE OF BIRTH	16 October 1980
BIRTHPLACE	Syosset, New York
DRAFT	2002 R1 Pick 1
HEIGHT	175 cm (5 ft 9 in)

SUE BIRD

An icon of the women's game, Sue Bird is the only player to win WNBA titles in three different decades — all won with Seattle Storm where she spent her 20-year career. A model of consistency, Bird was known for her ability to deliver the ball to the right team-mate at the right moment game after game and season after season.

CAREER POINTS
6,803

APG
5.6

PPG
11.7

ALL-STAR GAMES
13

WNBA MVP
0

ASSISTS
3,234

REBOUNDS
1,466

RPG
2.5

ACTIVE AREAS

SG
PF
PG
C
SF

As a testament to her longevity and all-round brilliance, Bird became the oldest player to complete a season in 2022 when she was 41 years and 246 days old. She also features in the top 10 greatest-ever players in 13 different categories, leading the lists in Most Seasons Played, Games Played, Assists, Minutes Played, All-Star Aappearances and Turnovers.

DID YOU KNOW?

Five-times Olympic gold medallist Bird was the flag-bearer for the US Olympic team in the opening ceremony of the Tokyo Games in 2021.

TOP 5 NOTABLE HONOURS

- 5x Olympic gold medal — Women's Basketball Team: (2004, 2008, 2012, 2016, 2020)
- 4x WNBA Champion: (2004, 2008, 2010, 2012)
- 1x WNBA Finals MVP: (2016)
- 5x All WNBA First Team: (2002—05, 2016)
- WNBA 10th, 15th, 20th, 25th Anniversary Team

8 24

TEAMS
LA Lakers (1996–2016)

POSITION	Sm. Forward/Sh. Guard
ACTIVE YEARS	1996–2016
DATE OF BIRTH	23 August 1978
BIRTHPLACE	Philadelphia, Pennsylvania
DRAFT	1996 R1 Pick 13
HEIGHT	192.1 cm (6 ft 6 in)

CAREER POINTS
33,643

APG
4.7

PPG
25.0

ALL-STAR GAMES
18

NBA MVP
1

ASSISTS
6,306

REBOUNDS
7,047

RPG
5.2

ACTIVE AREAS

SG PF PG C d SF

KOBE BRYANT

Considered basketball royalty, Kobe Bryant will forever hold a legendary status in the NBA. A warrior on the court, with his sublime footwork and an innate ability and courage to take the shot when the game was on the line, Bryant was simply flawless in offence.

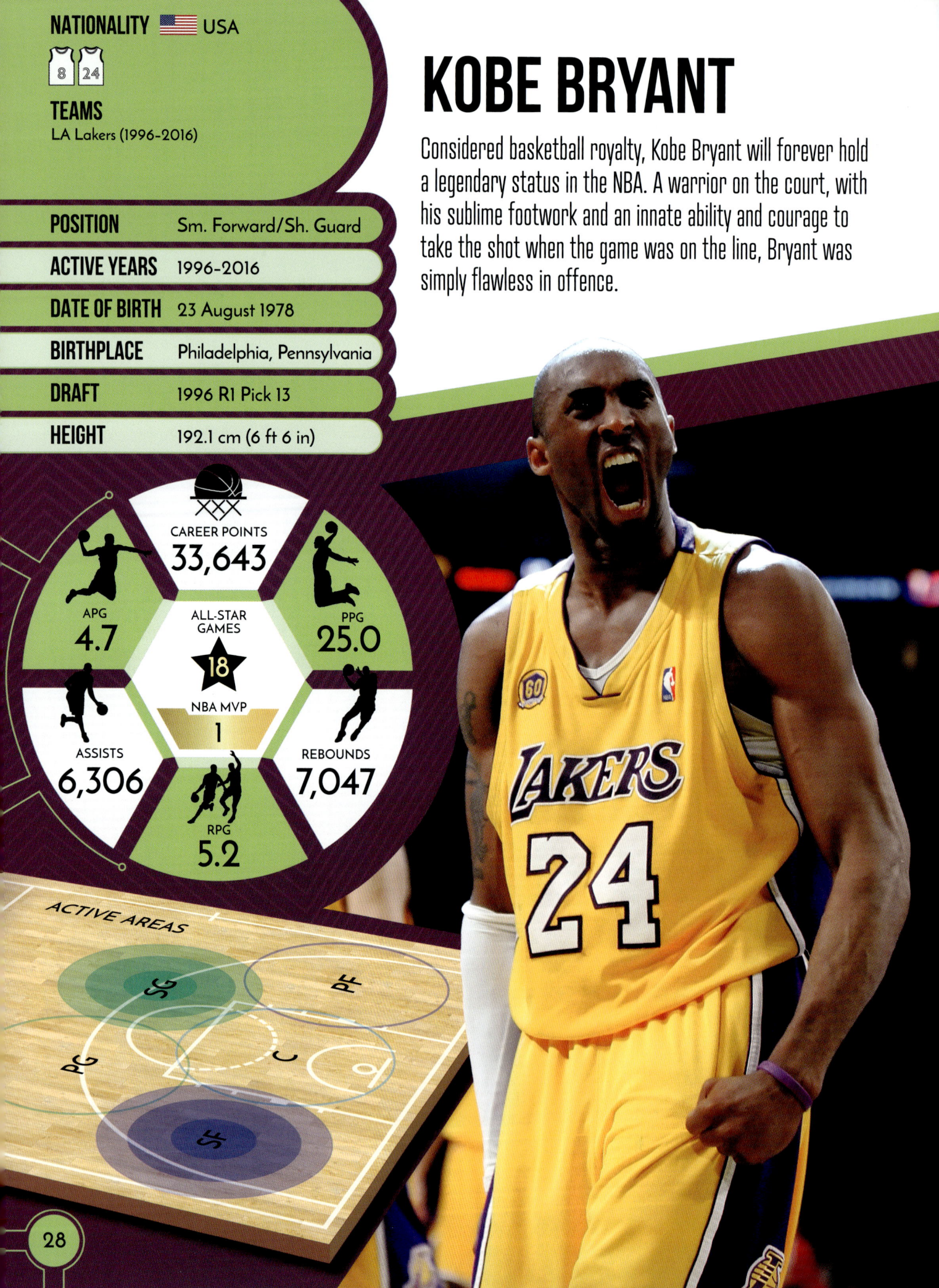

He spent his entire 20-year career with the LA Lakers, where he is the all-time leading points scorer. Tragically, Bryant died in a helicopter crash in January 2020.

TOP 5 NOTABLE HONOURS
- 2x Olympic gold medal — Men's Basketball Team: (2008, 2012)
- 5x NBA Champion: (2000, 2001, 2002, 2009, 2010)
- 2x NBA Finals MVP: (2009, 2010)
- 4x NBA All-Star Game MVP: (2002, 2007, 2009, 2011)
- NBA 75th Anniversary Team

DID YOU KNOW?
Kobe won an Academy Award for writing and narrating the animated short feature *Dear Basketball* in 2016.

15 | 25

TEAMS Toronto Raptors (1998-2004), New Jersey Nets (2004-09), Orlando Magic (2009-10), Phoenix Suns (2010-11), Dallas Mav'ks (2011-14), Memphis Grizzlies (2014-17), Sacramento Kings (2017-18), Atlanta Hawks (2018-20)

POSITION	Sh. Guard/Sm. Forward
ACTIVE YEARS	1998-2020
DATE OF BIRTH	26 January 1977
BIRTHPLACE	Daytona Beach, Florida
DRAFT	1998 R1 Pick 5
HEIGHT	192.12 cm (6 ft 6 in)

CAREER POINTS
25,728

APG
3.1

PPG
16.7

ALL-STAR GAMES
8

NBA MVP
0

ASSISTS
4,714

REBOUNDS
6,606

RPG
4.3

ACTIVE AREAS

SG · PF · PG · C · SF

VINCE CARTER

Once described as 'half man, half amazing', Vince Carter emulated the bouncy game of the great Michael Jordan, taking dunking to a superhuman level. With a career that spanned 22 years, Carter was a powerhouse of a player who could fulfil a number of roles for his teams.

A born entertainer, Carter was hugely popular with fans thanks to his leaping ability and slam dunks, which earned him the nicknames 'Vinsanity' and 'Air Canada'. Indeed, he has been ranked as the greatest-ever slam dunker by many fellow pros.

TOP 5 NOTABLE HONOURS
- 1x Olympic gold medal — Men's Basketball Team: (2000)
- 1x NBA Rookie of the Year: (1999)
- 1x NBA All-Rookie First Team: (1999)
- 1x NBA Slam Dunk Contest Champion: (2000)
- 1x NBA Sportsmanship Award: (2020)

DID YOU KNOW?
Vince Carter holds the unique record of being the only player in NBA history to play in four different decades: the 1990s, 2000s, 2010s and 2020s.

NATIONALITY 🇺🇸 USA

13

TEAMS Harlem Globetrotters (1958-59), Philadelphia/San Francisco Warriors (1959-65), Philadelphia 76ers (1965-68), LA Lakers (1968-73)

POSITION	Centre
ACTIVE YEARS	1958-1973
DATE OF BIRTH	21 August 1936
BIRTHPLACE	Philadelphia, Pennsylvania
DRAFT	1956
HEIGHT	215.9 cm (7 ft 1 in)

WILT CHAMBERLAIN

Multiple record holder, Wilt Chamberlain was one of the game's first superstars. An athletic specimen who could clear 1.98 metres in the high jump and run the 100 metres in under 11 seconds, Wilt was a force on court with his amazing reaction time. He scored three-quarters of his career points from rebounds!

CAREER POINTS
31,419

APG
4.4

PPG
30.1

ALL-STAR GAMES
13

NBA MVP
4

ASSISTS
4,643

REBOUNDS
23,924

RPG
22.9

ACTIVE AREAS

SG PF
PG C
SF

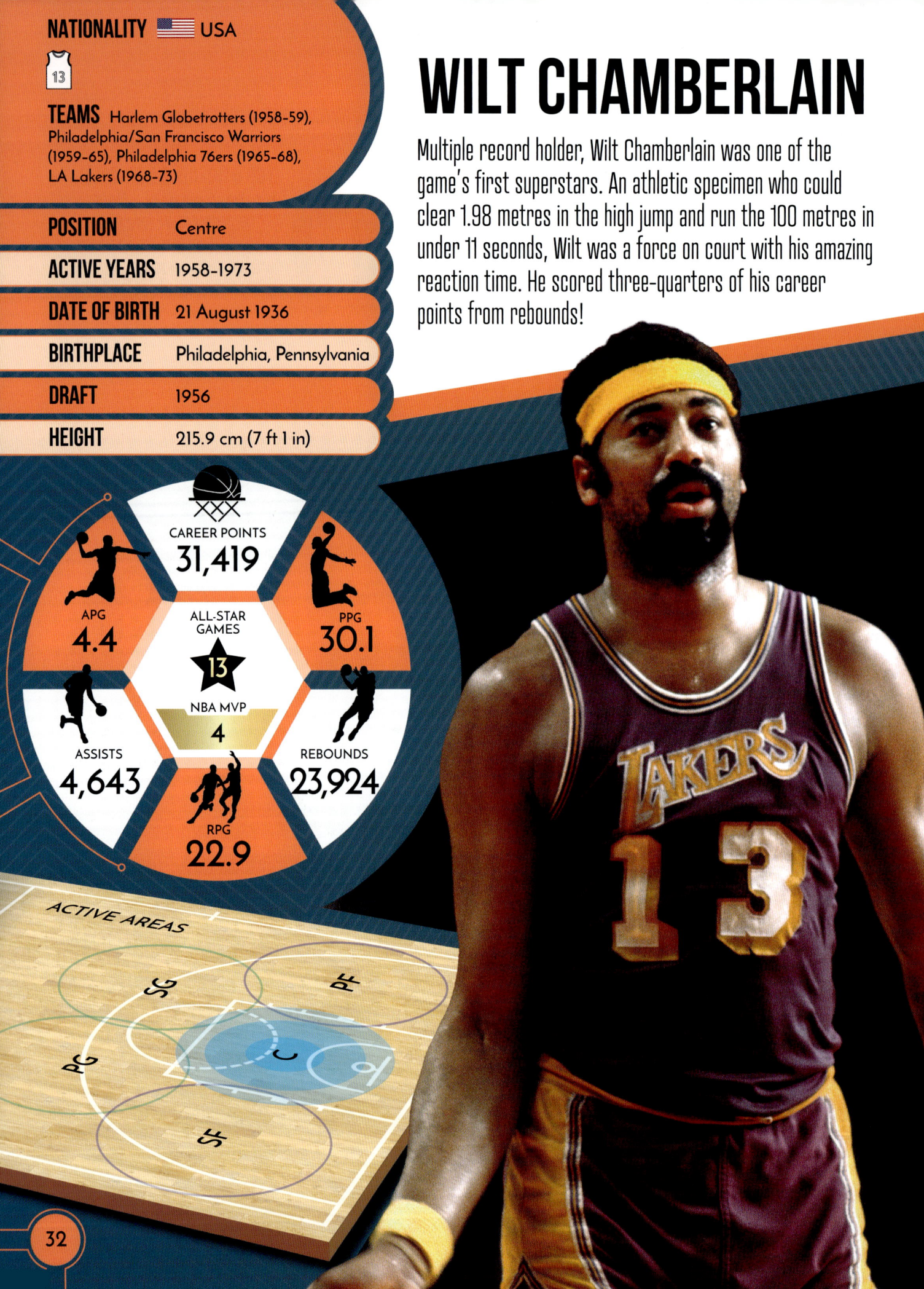

Chamberlain was a former member of the legendary Harlem Globetrotters team, where he made his NBA debut. In honour of this supremely gifted athlete, the Globetrotters retired his No.13 jersey in 2000.

TOP 5 NOTABLE HONOURS
- 2× NBA Champion: (1967, 1972)
- 1x NBA Finals MVP: (1972)
- 1x NBA All-Star Game MVP: (1960)
- NBA 35th, 50th and 75th Anniversary Team
- 7x NBA Scoring Champion: (1960—1966)

DID YOU KNOW?
In 1962, Chamberlain became the first player to score 100 points in a game, which took place against New York Knicks in Hershey, Pennsylvania.

30

TEAMS
Golden State Warriors (2009–)

POSITION	Point Guard
ACTIVE YEARS	2009-present
DATE OF BIRTH	14 March 1988
BIRTHPLACE	Akron, Ohio
DRAFT	Round 1, Pick 7
HEIGHT	187.96 cm (6 ft 2 in)

STEPHEN CURRY

He might be among the game's shorter superstars but Stephen Curry is also one of basketball's greatest shooters of all-time. He is famed for his ability to score three-point shots with unerring accuracy, which has inspired many up-and-coming players to copy his shooting technique.

CAREER POINTS
23,302

APG
6.4

PPG
24.8

ALL-STAR GAMES
10

NBA MVP
2

ASSISTS
6,031

REBOUNDS
4,436

RPG
4.7

ACTIVE AREAS

SG

PF

PG

C

SF

Curry has sublime ball-handling skills too, combined with great vision, playmaking amd passing, which have helped him win four NBA titles with the Golden State Warriors.

TOP 5 NOTABLE HONOURS
- 4x NBA Champion: (2015, 2017, 2018, 2022)
- 1x NBA Finals MVP: (2022)
- 1x NBA All-Star Game MVP: (2022)
- NBA 75th Anniversary Team
- 2x NBA Three-Point Contest Champion: (2015, 2021)

DID YOU KNOW?
Curry is one of the highest paid athletes in the world and considered by many as the current 'face of NBA'.

ADRIAN DANTLEY

NATIONALITY 🇺🇸 USA

44 4 45 7

TEAMS Buffalo Braves (1976-77), Indiana Pacers ('77), LA Lakers (1977-79), Utah Jazz (1979-86), Detroit Pistons (1986-89), Dallas M'vericks (1989-90), Mil'kee Bucks ('91), Aresium Milano (1991-92)

POSITION	Small Forward
ACTIVE YEARS	1976-1992
DATE OF BIRTH	28 February 1955
BIRTHPLACE	Akron, Ohio
DRAFT	1976 Round 1, Pick 6
HEIGHT	195.6 cm (6 ft 5 in)

Adrian Dantley is one of the NBA's best-ever free throw shooters, known for his set routine of four two-handed dribbles and two spins of the ball before every free throw! A clever player, he frequently dribbled the ball high to draw reach-in fouls and gain advantage in one-on-one situations.

CAREER POINTS
23,177

APG
3.0

ALL-STAR GAMES
★ 6

PPG
24.3

NBA MVP
0

ASSISTS
2,830

REBOUNDS
5,455

RPG
5.7

ACTIVE AREAS

PG SG C PF SF

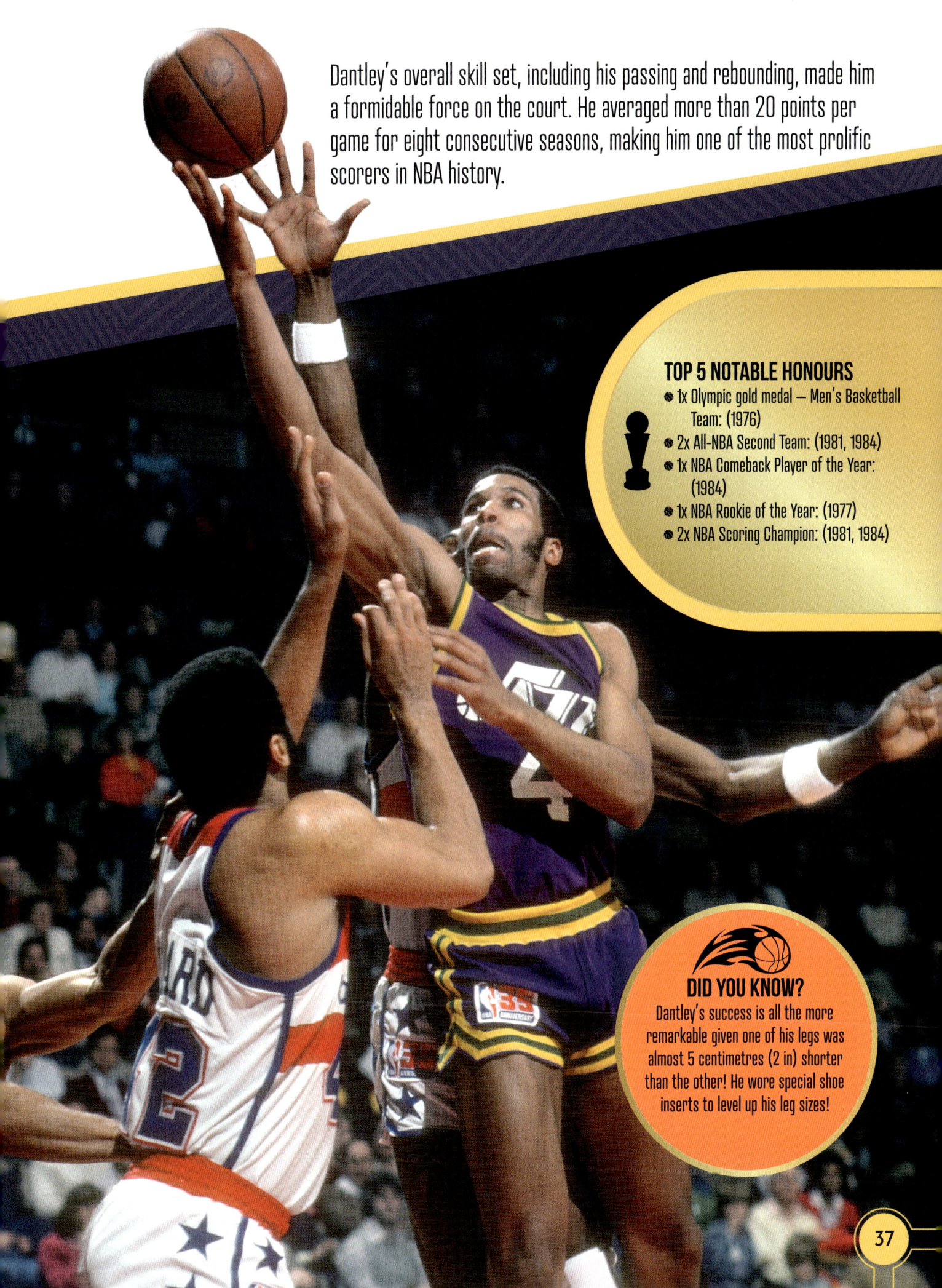

Dantley's overall skill set, including his passing and rebounding, made him a formidable force on the court. He averaged more than 20 points per game for eight consecutive seasons, making him one of the most prolific scorers in NBA history.

TOP 5 NOTABLE HONOURS

- 1x Olympic gold medal — Men's Basketball Team: (1976)
- 2x All-NBA Second Team: (1981, 1984)
- 1x NBA Comeback Player of the Year: (1984)
- 1x NBA Rookie of the Year: (1977)
- 2x NBA Scoring Champion: (1981, 1984)

DID YOU KNOW?

Dantley's success is all the more remarkable given one of his legs was almost 5 centimetres (2 in) shorter than the other! He wore special shoe inserts to level up his leg sizes!

NATIONALITY 🇺🇸 USA

TEAMS
Toronto Raptors (2009-18), San Antonio Spurs (2018-21) **Chicago Bulls (2021–)**

DEMAR DEROZAN

DeMar DeRozan has steadily amassed an impressive points total during his 14-year career to date. DeRozan is famous for his vision and lightning-quick power passes. Many believe he could have had a stellar career as an NFL quarterback had he not chosen basketball.

POSITION	Sh. Guard/Sm. Forward
ACTIVE YEARS	2009-present
DATE OF BIRTH	7 August 1989
BIRTHPLACE	Compton, California
DRAFT	2009 Round 1, Pick 9
HEIGHT	198.1 cm (6 ft 6 in)

CAREER POINTS
23,201

APG
4.0

PPG
21.2

ALL-STAR GAMES
6

NBA MVP
0

ASSISTS
4,448

REBOUNDS
4,851

RPG
4.4

ACTIVE AREAS

SG

PF

PG

C

SF

A prolific mid-range shooter with faultless footwork, DeRozan has perfected his art and become one of the best at scoring inside the arc with a broad variety of shots.

TOP 5 NOTABLE HONOURS
- 1x Olympic gold medal — Men's Basketball Team: (2016)
- 1x FIBA World Basketball gold medal: (2014)
- 1x First-team Parade All-American: (2008)
- 1x NBA All-Star Rising Star: (2011)
- 2x All-NBA Second Team: 2018, 2022

DID YOU KNOW?
DeRozan's nickname is 'Deebo', which comes from a character in the 1995 film *Friday* played by Tommy Lister Jr.

NATIONALITY 🇺🇸 USA

22

TEAMS
Portland Trail Blazers (1983-95),
Houston Rockets (1995-98)

POSITION	Sh. Guard/Sm. Forward
ACTIVE YEARS	1983-1998
DATE OF BIRTH	22 June 1962
BIRTHPLACE	New Orleans, Louisiana
DRAFT	1983 Round 1, Pick 14
HEIGHT	200.7 cm (6 ft 7 in)

CAREER POINTS
22,195

APG
5.6

PPG
20.4

ALL-STAR GAMES
10

NBA MVP
0

ASSISTS
6,125

REBOUNDS
6,677

RPG
6.1

ACTIVE AREAS

SG

PF

PG

C

SF

CLYDE DREXLER

One of NBA's greatest-ever shooting guards, Clyde Drexler — nicknamed 'Clyde the Glide'— was known for being a supremely graceful player. He possessed an explosive first step that allowed him to make his seemingly effortless high-flying swoops on the basket.

Drexler enjoyed a brilliant 15-year career, mostly with Portland Trail Blazers who retired his No.22 shirt after his 11 years with the team. This smooth, powerhouse of a player influenced a generation.

TOP 5 NOTABLE HONOURS
- 1x Olympic gold medal – Men's Basketball Team: (1992)
- 1x NBA champion: (1995)
- 1x All-NBA First Team: (1992)
- NBA 50th and 75th Anniversary Team
- Texas Sports Hall of Fame inductee in 1998

DID YOU KNOW?
Drexler was part of the 1992 Olympic gold medal Dream Team along with superstars Larry Bird, Magic Johnson, Karl Malone, Patrick Ewing, Charles Barkley, Scottie Pippen and the great Michael Jordan.

41

NATIONALITY 🇺🇸 USA

21

TEAMS
San Antonio Spurs (1997–2016)

POSITION	Pw. Forward/Centre
ACTIVE YEARS	1997–2016
DATE OF BIRTH	25 April 1976
BIRTHPLACE	Saint Croix, US Virgin Islands
DRAFT	1997 R1 Pick 1
HEIGHT	210.8 cm (6 ft 11 in)

TIM DUNCAN

Described as the consummate professional and a model team player, Tim Duncan was never the showman but had a disciplined approach to the game. He excelled in scoring, rebounding, shot-blocking and playmaking, making him influential on both ends of the court.

CAREER POINTS
26,496

APG
3.0

PPG
19.0

ALL-STAR GAMES
15

NBA MVP
2

ASSISTS
4,225

REBOUNDS
15,091

RPG
10.8

ACTIVE AREAS

SG
PF
PG
C
SF

He was San Antonio Spurs' No.1 draft pick for 1997 — the team he stayed with for his entire career, later becoming a mentor for younger teammates and instilling in them the qualities that made him a winner and NBA giant.

TOP 5 NOTABLE HONOURS
- 5x NBA Champion: (1999, 2003, 2005, 2007, 2014)
- 3x NBA Finals MVP: (1999, 2003, 2005)
- 10x All-NBA First Team (1998–2005, 2007, 2013)
- 1x NBA Rookie of the Year: (1998)
- NBA 75th Anniversary Team

DID YOU KNOW?
Tim Duncan's older sisters Cheryl and Tricia were champion swimmers — Tricia represented the US Virgin Island at the 1988 Olympics.

NATIONALITY 🇺🇸 USA

| 35 | 7 |

TEAMS Seattle SuperSonics/Oklahoma City Thunder (2007-16), Golden State Warriors (2016-19), Brooklyn Nets (2019-23), **Phoenix Suns (2023–)**

POSITION	Pw. Forward/Sm. Forward
ACTIVE YEARS	2007-present
DATE OF BIRTH	29 September 1988
BIRTHPLACE	Washington DC
DRAFT	2007 R1 Pick 2
HEIGHT	210.8 cm (6 ft 11 in)

KEVIN DURANT

Nicknamed 'The Durantula', Kevin Durant is a devastating scorer, be it shooting at range, driving and finishing at the bucket, executing mid-range shots or converting with his back to the bucket. He may not be the most graceful player, but his power and precision make him the most potent scorer in the NBA today.

CAREER POINTS
28,564

APG
4.4

PPG
27.3

ALL-STAR GAMES
14

NBA MVP
1

ASSISTS
4,585

REBOUNDS
7,351

RPG
7.0

ACTIVE AREAS

SG

PF

PG

C

SF

Now with the Phoenix Suns, Durant has passed 1,000 NBA starts and amassed incredible stats along the way. He is likely to cement his place in the list of all-time top scorers by the time he calls time on a stellar career.

DID YOU KNOW?
Kevin Durant likes to play video games and his favourite is the first-person shooter series *Call Of Duty!*

TOP 5 NOTABLE HONOURS
- 2x NBA Champion: (2017, 2018)
- 3x Olympic gold medal – Men's Basketball Team: (2012, 2016, 2020)
- 6x All-NBA First Team: (2010–2014, 2018)
- 4x NBA Scoring Champion: 2010, 2011, 2012, 2014
- 2x NBA All-Star Game MVP: 2012, 2019

23 **22** **2**

TEAMS Milwaukee Bucks (1976-78), Indiana Pacers (1978-80), Denver Nuggets (1980-90), Dallas Mavericks (1990-91), Basket Napoli (1991-92)

POSITION	Small Forward
ACTIVE YEARS	1976-1992
DATE OF BIRTH	5 January 1954
BIRTHPLACE	Columbia, South Carolina
DRAFT	1976 R2 Pick 23
HEIGHT	203.2 cm (6 ft 8 in)

ALEX ENGLISH

It was in the 1980s that Alex English became an NBA superstar with the Denver Nuggets. A master of the mid-range game, there was no one better at getting off shots in the crowded key area. In fact, he scored more points than anyone during that era.

CAREER POINTS
25,613

APG
3.6

PPG
21.5

ALL-STAR GAMES
8

NBA MVP
0

ASSISTS
4,351

REBOUNDS
6,538

RPG
5.5

ACTIVE AREAS

SG
PF
PG
C
SF

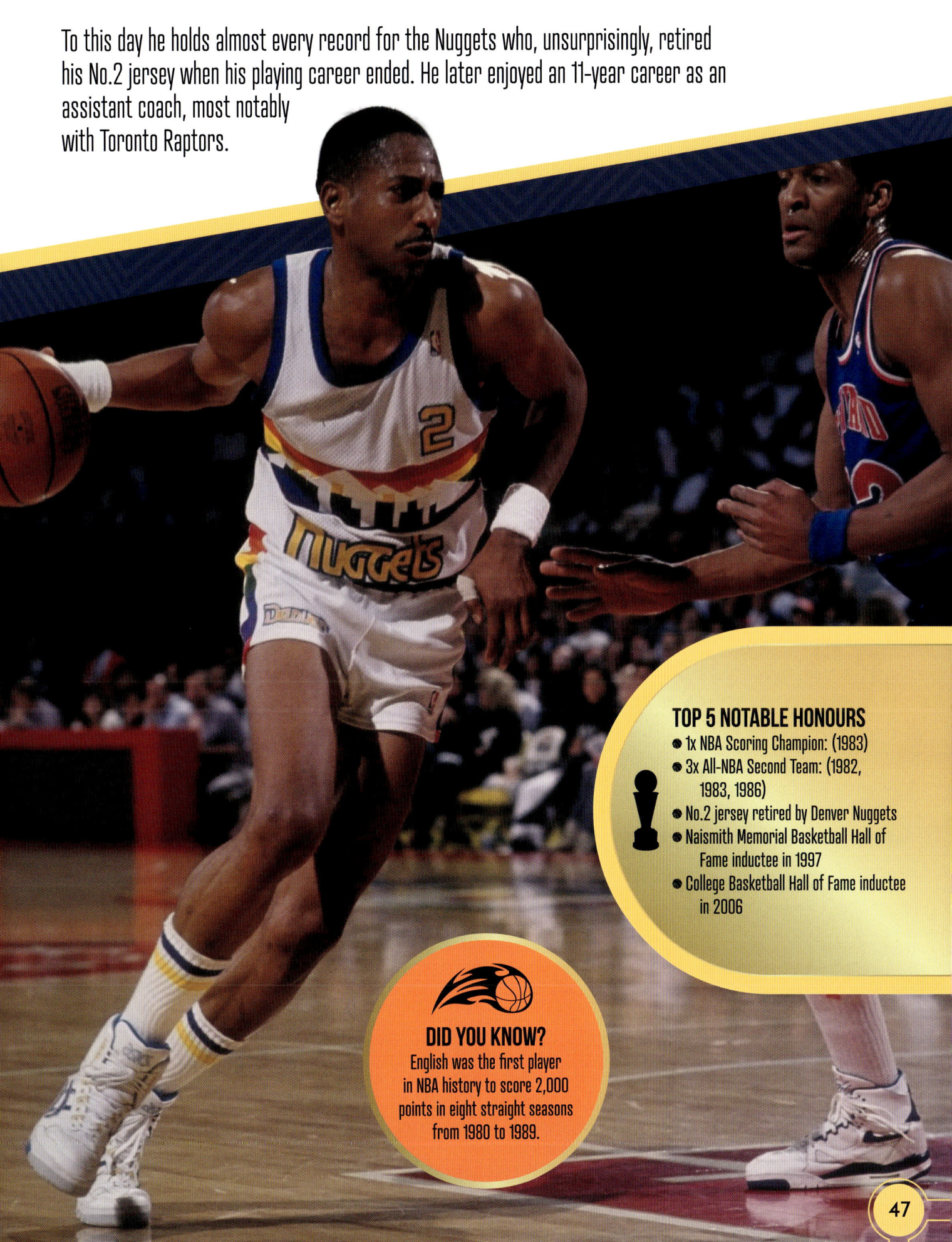

To this day he holds almost every record for the Nuggets who, unsurprisingly, retired his No.2 jersey when his playing career ended. He later enjoyed an 11-year career as an assistant coach, most notably with Toronto Raptors.

TOP 5 NOTABLE HONOURS
- 1x NBA Scoring Champion: (1983)
- 3x All-NBA Second Team: (1982, 1983, 1986)
- No.2 jersey retired by Denver Nuggets
- Naismith Memorial Basketball Hall of Fame inductee in 1997
- College Basketball Hall of Fame inductee in 2006

DID YOU KNOW?
English was the first player in NBA history to score 2,000 points in eight straight seasons from 1980 to 1989.

32 6

TEAMS
Virginia Squires (1971-73), New York Nets (1973-76), Philadelphia 76ers (1976-87)

POSITION	Small Forward
ACTIVE YEARS	1971-1987 (ABA & NBA)
DATE OF BIRTH	22 February 1950
BIRTHPLACE	Roosevelt, New York
DRAFT	1972 R1 Pick 12
HEIGHT	200.7 cm (6 ft 7 in)

JULIUS ERVING

Among the most exciting players ever to have graced the NBA, Julius Erving — known affectionately as 'Dr J' — was a phenomenal talent, who thrilled fans with his explosive style.

CAREER POINTS
30,026

APG
4.2

PPG
24.2

ALL-STAR GAMES
⭐ **11**

NBA MVP
1

ASSISTS
5,176

REBOUNDS
10,525

RPG
8.5

ACTIVE AREAS

SG

PF

PG

C

SF

Powerful, fast, and willing to take risks, there was no finer sight than Erving leaping with the ball in one hand, balletically soaring through the air before slam dunking with effortless grace and force — many believe he is the greatest dunker of all-time. He was only the third professional player to pass the 30,000 points-mark and is rightly regarded as an NBA great.

TOP 5 NOTABLE HONOURS
- 1x NBA Champion: (1983)
- 2× NBA All-Star Game MVP: (1977, 1983)
- NBA 35th, 50th and 75th Anniversary Team
- ABA* All-Time Team
- ABA All-time MVP

* The American Basketball Association (ABA) was another elite men's professional basketball league that ran from 1967 to 1976. The ABA merged into the NBA in 1976.

DID YOU KNOW?
Dr J's most famous play was against the LA Lakers in 1983 when he stole possession, raced towards the arc, cupped the ball into his wrist and forearm, before taking off for a slam dunk described as 'Rock the Baby'.

NATIONALITY 🇯🇲 Jamaica

| 33 | 6 |

TEAMS
New York Knicks (1985-2000)
Seattle SuperSonics (2000-01)
Orlando Magic (2001-02)

POSITION	Centre
ACTIVE YEARS	1985-2002
DATE OF BIRTH	5 August 1962
BIRTHPLACE	Kingston, Jamaica
DRAFT	1985 R1 Pick 1
HEIGHT	213.4 cm (7 ft)

CAREER POINTS
24,815

APG
1.9

PPG
21.0

ALL-STAR GAMES
11

NBA MVP
0

ASSISTS
2,215

REBOUNDS
11,617

RPG
9.8

ACTIVE AREAS

SG
PF
PG
C
SF

PATRICK EWING

Patrick Ewing was a gifted football and cricket player while he lived in Jamaica, but at the age of 11, when his family relocated to Boston, he began impressing with a basketball at high school and the rest is history.

With his imposing physical presence, Ewing was an unstoppable force at college where he is regarded as one of the all-time best. He would spend most of his career playing for New York Knicks and holds the team's all-time records for points, rebounds, blocks and steals.

TOP 5 NOTABLE HONOURS

- 2x Olympic gold medal – Men's Basketball Team: (1984, 1992)
- 1x All-NBA First Team: (1990)
- 1x NBA All-Rookie Team: (1986)
- NBA 50th and 75th Anniversary Team
- No.33 retired by New York Knicks

DID YOU KNOW?

In 1999, Ewing became just the 10th player in NBA history to record both 22,000 points and 10,000 rebounds.

NATIONALITY 🇺🇸 USA

21 **5** **2**

TEAMS
Minnesota Timberwolves (1995-2007), (2015-16),
Boston Celtics (2007-13),
Brooklyn Nets (2013-15)

POSITION	Power Forward
ACTIVE YEARS	1995-2016
DATE OF BIRTH	19 May 1976
BIRTHPLACE	Greenville, South Carolina
DRAFT	1995 R1 Pick 5
HEIGHT	210.8 cm (6 ft 11 in)

KEVIN GARNETT

An imposing presence on the court, Kevin Garnett was a powerful, athletic and dominant player. A prolific rebounder, he was also incredible on defence, able to block shots, break through screens and win games for his team.

CAREER POINTS
26,071

APG
3.7

PPG
17.8

ALL-STAR GAMES
15

NBA MVP
1

ASSISTS
5,445

REBOUNDS
14,662

RPG
10.0

ACTIVE AREAS

SG

PF

PG

C

SF

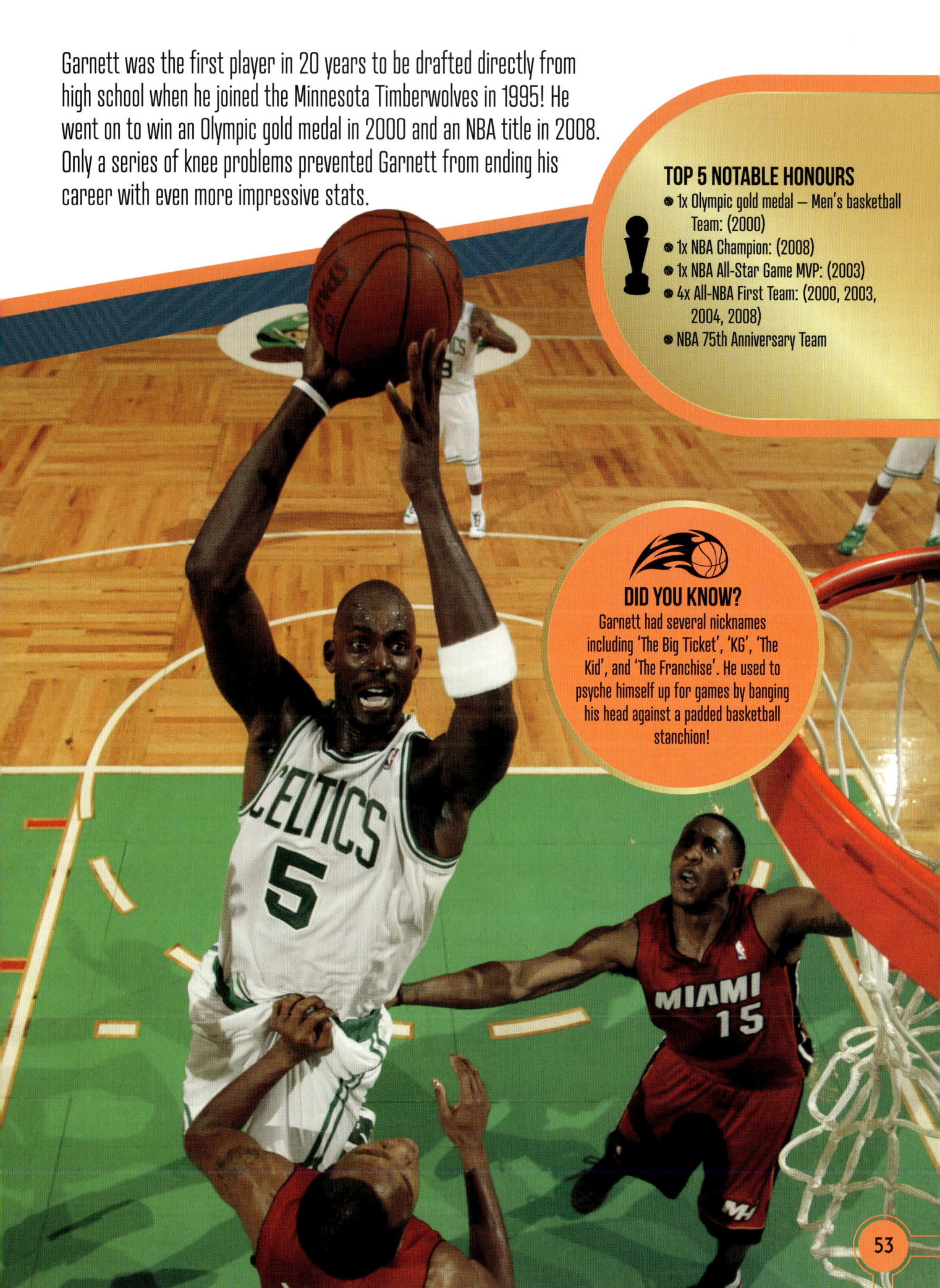

Garnett was the first player in 20 years to be drafted directly from high school when he joined the Minnesota Timberwolves in 1995! He went on to win an Olympic gold medal in 2000 and an NBA title in 2008. Only a series of knee problems prevented Garnett from ending his career with even more impressive stats.

TOP 5 NOTABLE HONOURS
- 1x Olympic gold medal – Men's basketball Team: (2000)
- 1x NBA Champion: (2008)
- 1x NBA All-Star Game MVP: (2003)
- 4x All-NBA First Team: (2000, 2003, 2004, 2008)
- NBA 75th Anniversary Team

DID YOU KNOW?
Garnett had several nicknames including 'The Big Ticket', 'KG', 'The Kid', and 'The Franchise'. He used to psyche himself up for games by banging his head against a padded basketball stanchion!

NATIONALITY 🇺🇸 USA

15

TEAMS
Syracuse Nationals/Philadelphia 76ers
(1958-73)

POSITION	Sh. Guard/Po. Guard
ACTIVE YEARS	1958-1973
DATE OF BIRTH	26 June 1936
BIRTHPLACE	Huntingdon, West Virginia
DRAFT	1958 R2 Pick 14
HEIGHT	187.9 cm (6 ft 2 in)

HAL GREER

Hal Greer was a guard who was considered one of the very best in the 1960s, most admired for his speed and ability as a mid-range jumper. Greer possessed a unique free throw technique that set him apart from other players.

CAREER POINTS
21,586

APG
4.0

PPG
19.2

ALL-STAR GAMES
10

NBA MVP
0

ASSISTS
4,540

REBOUNDS
5,665

RPG
5.0

ACTIVE AREAS

SG

PF

PG

C

SF

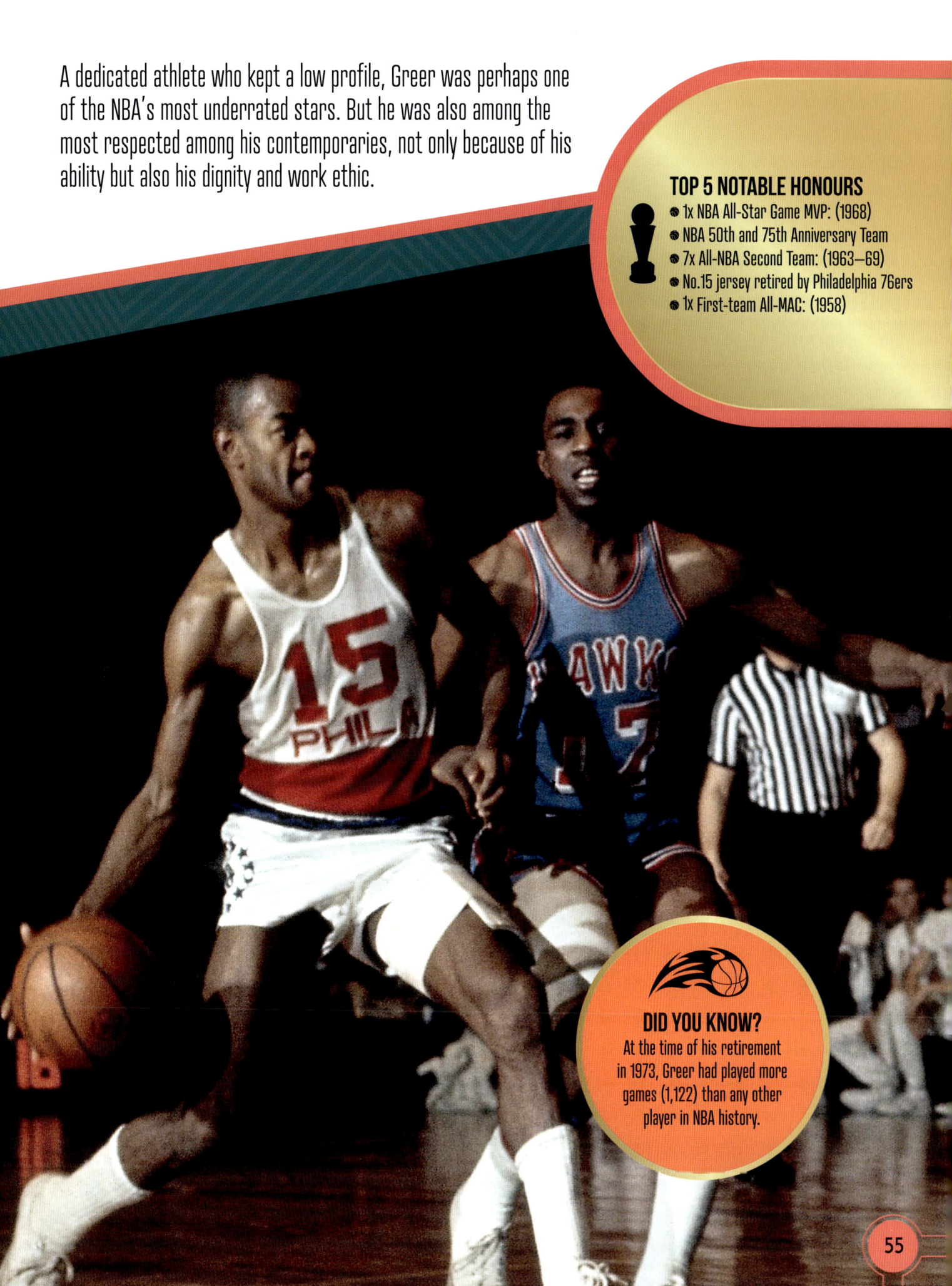

A dedicated athlete who kept a low profile, Greer was perhaps one of the NBA's most underrated stars. But he was also among the most respected among his contemporaries, not only because of his ability but also his dignity and work ethic.

TOP 5 NOTABLE HONOURS
- 1x NBA All-Star Game MVP: (1968)
- NBA 50th and 75th Anniversary Team
- 7x All-NBA Second Team: (1963–69)
- No.15 jersey retired by Philadelphia 76ers
- 1x First-team All-MAC: (1958)

DID YOU KNOW?
At the time of his retirement in 1973, Greer had played more games (1,122) than any other player in NBA history.

JAMES HARDEN

James Harden is the highest left-handed scorer of all time. He is famed for his ball dominance and has perfected the art of the 'step-back threes', amassing an impressive three-point field goal percentage of 36.4 across a career now into its 15th season.

NATIONALITY 🇺🇸 USA

13 1

TEAMS Oklahoma City Thunder (2009-12), Houston Rockets (2012-21), Brooklyn Nets (2021-22), Philadelphia 76ers (2022-23) **LA Clippers (2023–)**

POSITION	Sh. Guard/Po. Guard
ACTIVE YEARS	2009-present
DATE OF BIRTH	26 August 1989
BIRTHPLACE	Los Angeles, California
DRAFT	2009, R1 Pick 3
HEIGHT	195.6 cm (6 ft 5 in)

CAREER POINTS
25,721

APG
7.1

PPG
24.3

ALL-STAR GAMES
10

NBA MVP
1

ASSISTS
7,506

REBOUNDS
5,950

RPG
5.6

ACTIVE AREAS

SG

PF

PG

C

SF

Occasionally criticised for being too predictable, his presence on the court nevertheless drives his teammates on, upping the tenor and energy levels with his playmaking and assists.

TOP 5 NOTABLE HONOURS

- 1x Olympic gold medal – Men's Basketball Team: (2012)
- 6x All-NBA First Team: (2014, 2015, 2017–2020)
- 1x NBA Sixth Man of the Year: (2012)
- 3× NBA Scoring Champion (2018, 2019, 2020)
- NBA 75th Anniversary Team

DID YOU KNOW?

Harden's four-year contract extension with the Houston Rockets in July 2017 made his six-year deal worth a guaranteed $228 million (£175 million) – the biggest in NBA history at the time.

NATIONALITY 🇺🇸 USA

17

TEAMS
Boston Celtics

JOHN HAVLICEK

A forward with immense stamina, John Havlicek spent his entire 16-year professional career with Boston Celtics. A tireless worker, he was happy to keep out of the spotlight and give every ounce of his energy to the team's cause.

POSITION	Sm. Forward/Sh. Guard
ACTIVE YEARS	1962-1978
DATE OF BIRTH	8 April 1940
BIRTHPLACE	Martins Ferry, Ohio
DRAFT	1962, R1 Pick 7
HEIGHT	195.6 cm (6 ft 5 in)

CAREER POINTS
26,395

APG
4.8

PPG
20.8

ALL-STAR GAMES
13

NBA MVP
0

ASSISTS
6,114

REBOUNDS
8,007

RPG
6.3

ACTIVE AREAS

SG

PF

PG

C

SF

Intelligent and sharp on the court, his endurance was the stuff of legend, with few players able to match his fitness and intensity. He was an NBA champion no fewer than eight times and selected 13 times as an NBA All-Star, which underlines his reputation as one of the sport's greatest-ever all-rounders.

TOP 5 NOTABLE HONOURS
- 8x NBA Champion: (1963–1966, 1968, 1969, 1974, 1976)
- NBA 35th, 50th and 75th Anniversary Team
- 4x All-NBA First Team: (1971–1974)
- 5x NBA All-Defensive First Team: (1972–1976)
- 1x NBA All-Rookie First Team: (1963)

DID YOU KNOW?
Havlicek was a major early investor in the fast food chain Wendy's — which was the third largest behind McDonald's and Burger King as of 2018.

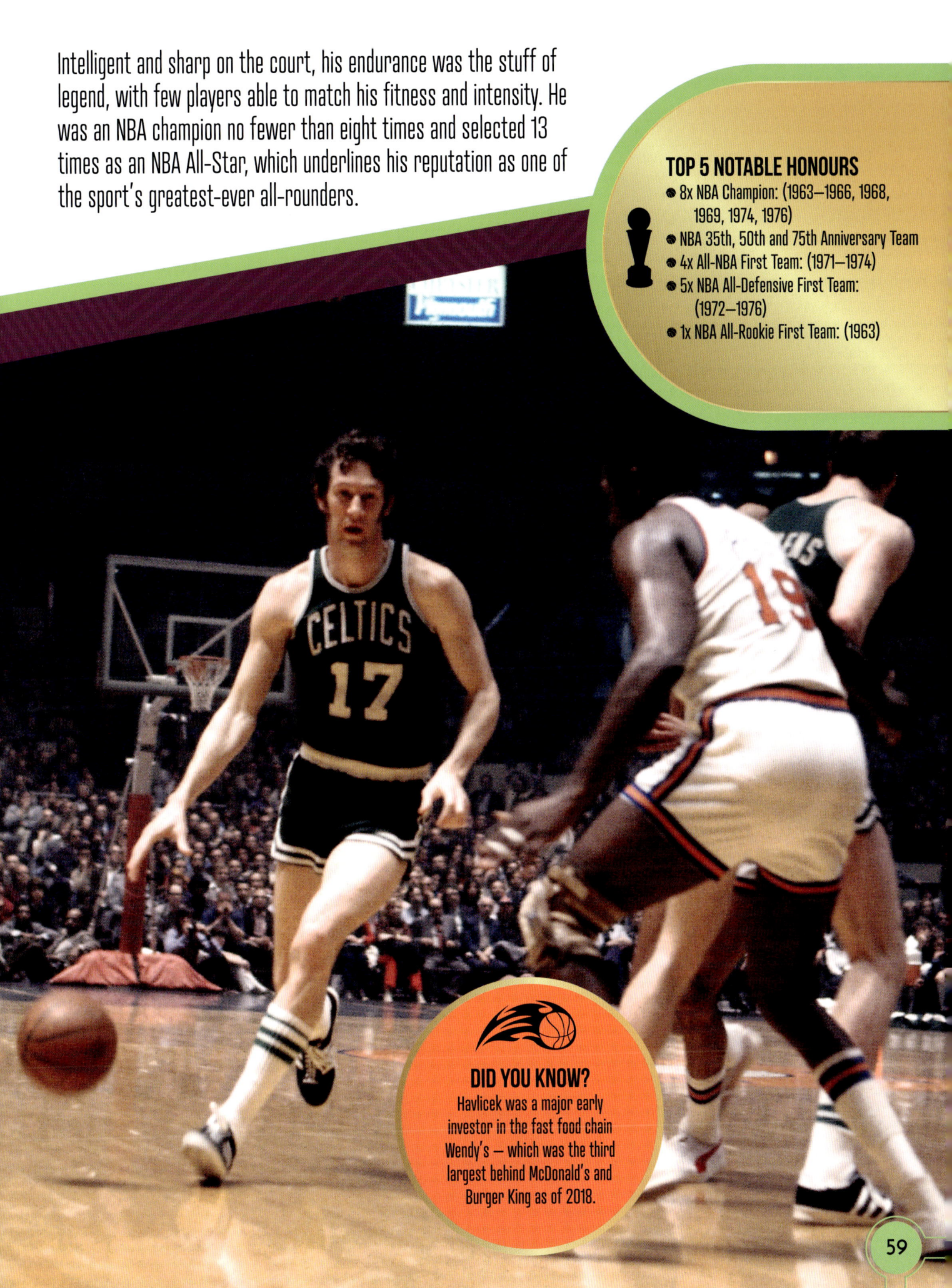

NATIONALITY 🇺🇸 USA

11 44

TEAMS
San Diego/Houston Rockets (1968-72),
Baltimore/Capital/Washington Bullets (1972-81),
Houston Rockets (1981-84)

POSITION	Pw. Forward/Centre
ACTIVE YEARS	1968-1984
DATE OF BIRTH	17 November 1945
BIRTHPLACE	Rayville, Louisiana
DRAFT	1968, R1 Pick 1
HEIGHT	205.7 cm (6 ft 9 in)

ELVIN HAYES

A supreme talent and athlete, Elvin Hayes was the superstar of his day who led Washington to the NBA title in 1978. An immensely powerful forward, he was famed for his trademark turnaround jumper and an aggressive defence that saw him top many NBA leaderboards during his career.

CAREER POINTS
27,313

APG
1.8

PPG
21.0

ALL-STAR GAMES
12

NBA MVP
0

ASSISTS
2,398

REBOUNDS
16,279

RPG
12.5

ACTIVE AREAS

SG PF

PG C

SF

60

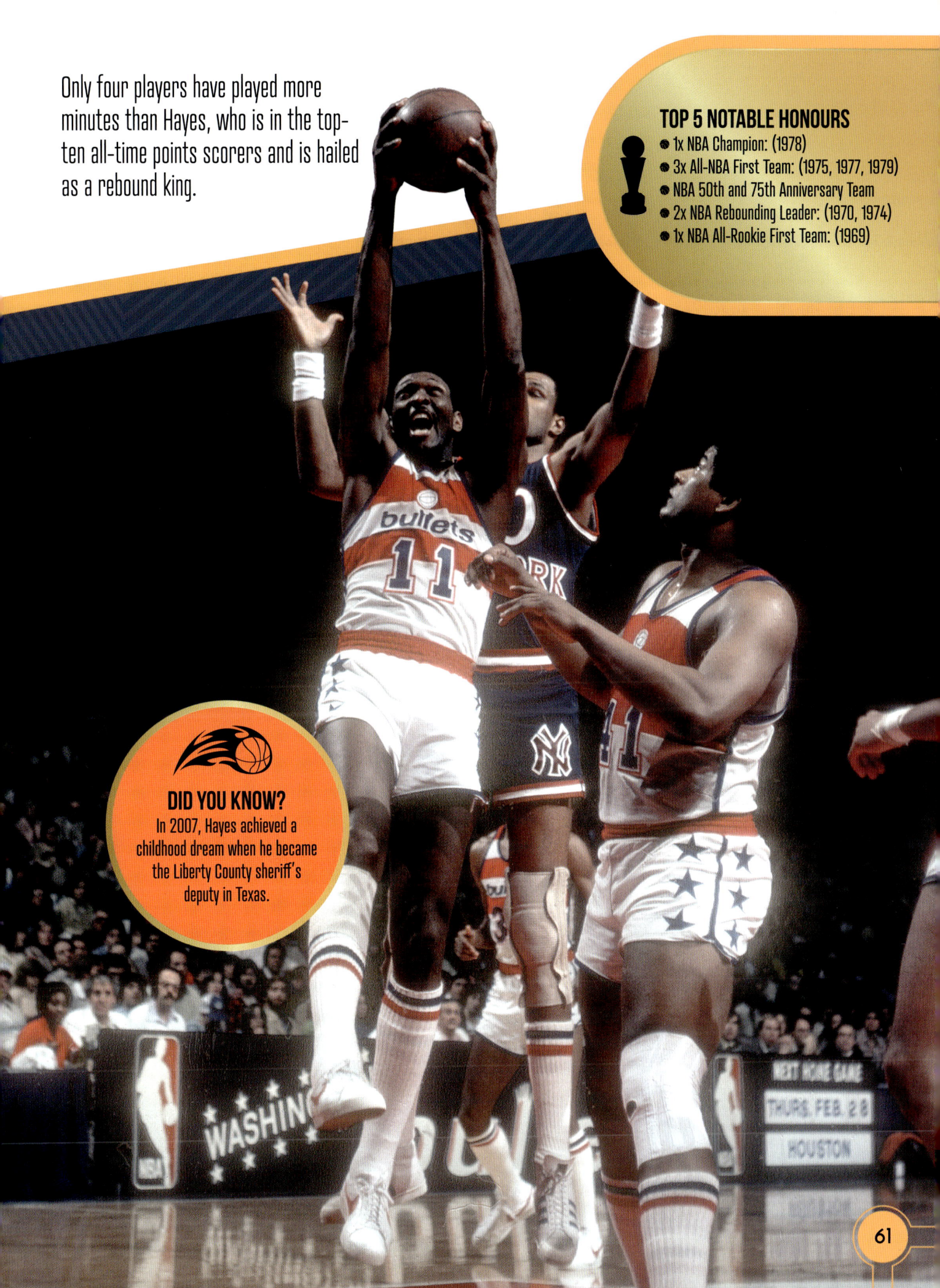

Only four players have played more minutes than Hayes, who is in the top-ten all-time points scorers and is hailed as a rebound king.

DID YOU KNOW?
In 2007, Hayes achieved a childhood dream when he became the Liberty County sheriff's deputy in Texas.

NATIONALITY USA

3 **1**

TEAMS Philadelphia 76ers (1996–2006), (2009–10), Denver Nuggets (2006–08), Detroit Pistons (2008–09), Memphis Grizzlies (2009) *Abroad:* Beşiktaş J.K. (2010–11)

POSITION	Sh. Guard/Po. Guard
ACTIVE YEARS	1996–2011
DATE OF BIRTH	7 June 1975
BIRTHPLACE	Hampton, Virginia
DRAFT	1996, R1 Pick 1
HEIGHT	182.9 cm (6 ft)

ALLEN IVERSEN

At just under 183 centimetres tall, Allen Iversen is one of the shortest NBA legends to have made his mark on the game. Nicknamed 'The Answer', Iversen used his shorter stature to his advantage and developed a style that made him quick, strong and agile on the court with a killer crossover move.

CAREER POINTS
24,368

APG
6.2

PPG
26.7

ALL-STAR GAMES
11

NBA MVP
1

ASSISTS
5,624

REBOUNDS
3,394

RPG
3.7

ACTIVE AREAS

SG   PF

PG   C

SF

He had a wonderful 17-season playing career, with his most productive period undoubtedly with the Philadelphia 76ers.

TOP 5 NOTABLE HONOURS
- 2x NBA All-Star Game MVP: (2001, 2005)
- 3x All-NBA First Team: (1999, 2001, 2005)
- NBA 75th Anniversary Team
- 4x NBA Scoring Champion: (1999, 2001, 2002, 2005)
- 1x Olympic bronze medal — Men's Basketball Team (2004)

LEBRON JAMES

LeBron James has scored more NBA points than any other player during a spectacular career. Starting with the Cleveland Cavaliers, James controversially moved to Miami Heat in 2010 to become an NBA champion. But he returned to the Cavaliers in 2014 and helped them become champions before heading to LA Lakers, his current team.

NATIONALITY 🇺🇸 USA

23 | **6**

TEAMS
Cleveland Cavaliers (2003-10, 2014-18),
Miami Heat (2010-14),
LA Lakers (2018–)

POSITION	Sm. Forward/Pw. Forward
ACTIVE YEARS	2003-present
DATE OF BIRTH	30 December 1984
BIRTHPLACE	Akron, Ohio
DRAFT	2003, R1 Pick 1
HEIGHT	205.7 cm (6 ft 9 in)

CAREER POINTS
40,114

APG
7.3

PPG
27.1

ALL-STAR GAMES
20

NBA MVP
4

ASSISTS
10,886

REBOUNDS
11,083

RPG
7.5

ACTIVE AREAS

SG

PF

PG

C

SF

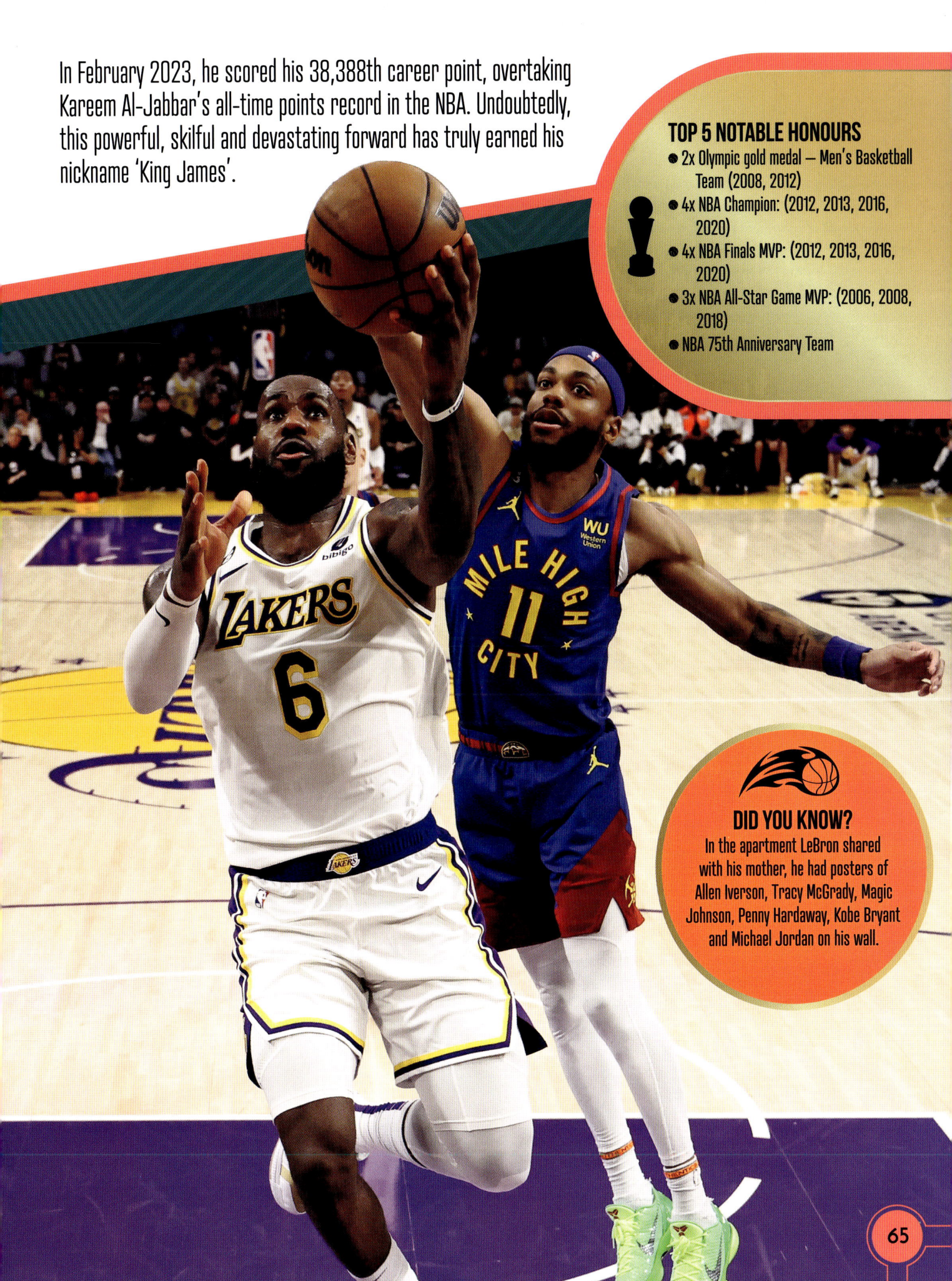

In February 2023, he scored his 38,388th career point, overtaking Kareem Al-Jabbar's all-time points record in the NBA. Undoubtedly, this powerful, skilful and devastating forward has truly earned his nickname 'King James'.

TOP 5 NOTABLE HONOURS

- 2x Olympic gold medal – Men's Basketball Team (2008, 2012)
- 4x NBA Champion: (2012, 2013, 2016, 2020)
- 4x NBA Finals MVP: (2012, 2013, 2016, 2020)
- 3x NBA All-Star Game MVP: (2006, 2008, 2018)
- NBA 75th Anniversary Team

DID YOU KNOW?

In the apartment LeBron shared with his mother, he had posters of Allen Iverson, Tracy McGrady, Magic Johnson, Penny Hardaway, Kobe Bryant and Michael Jordan on his wall.

32

TEAMS
LA Lakers (1979–1991, 1996)

POSITION	Po. Guard/Sh. Guard
ACTIVE YEARS	1979–1992, 1996
DATE OF BIRTH	14 August 1959
BIRTHPLACE	Lansing, Michigan
DRAFT	1979, R1 Pick 1
HEIGHT	205.7 cm (6 ft 9 in)

MAGIC JOHNSON

One of the first NBA stars to find worldwide fame, Magic Johnson was a joy to watch. Powerful, fast and devastating at times, there was no pass or shot he wouldn't attempt. Some of his assists were off the charts — blessed with an ability to find a teammate almost unlike any other player who had come before him.

CAREER POINTS
17,707

APG
11.2

PPG
19.5

ALL-STAR GAMES
12

NBA MVP
3

ASSISTS
10,141

REBOUNDS
6,559

RPG
7.2

ACTIVE AREAS

SG · PF · PG · C · P · SF

His personality oozed charm and he became a basketball superstar as a result. A truly gifted, wonderful athlete who took the game to another level, inspiring a whole generation along the way.

DID YOU KNOW?
Though his real name is Earvin Johnson, he was nicknamed 'Magic' during his days playing for Everett High School in Michigan by a journalist called Fred Stabley Junior.

TOP 5 NOTABLE HONOURS
- Olympic gold medal – Men's Basketball Team: (1992)
- 5x NBA Champion: (1980, 1982, 1985, 1987, 1988)
- 3x NBA Finals MVP: (1980, 1982, 1987)
- 2x NBA All-Star Game MVP: (1990, 1992)
- NBA 50th and 75th Anniversary Team

NATIONALITY 🇺🇸 USA

| 23 | 12 | 45 |

TEAMS
Chicago Bulls (1984-93), (1995-98)
Washington Wizards (2001-03)

POSITION	Sh. Guard/Sm. Forward
ACTIVE YEARS	1984-1993, 1995-1998, 2001-2003
DATE OF BIRTH	17 February 1963
BIRTHPLACE	New York, New York
DRAFT	1984 R1 Pick 3
HEIGHT	198.1 cm (6 ft 6 in)

MICHAEL JORDAN

Michael Jordan is regarded by many as the G.O.A.T (Greatest Of All Time) for his outstanding contribution to the sport. Responsible for spreading the NBA brand around the globe, he was a supreme athlete and an incredible basketballer whose ability to jump and slam dunk earned him the nicknames 'Air Jordan' and 'His Airness'.

CAREER POINTS
32,292

APG
5.3

PPG
30.1

ALL-STAR GAMES
14

NBA MVP
5

ASSISTS
5,633

REBOUNDS
6,672

RPG
6.2

ACTIVE AREAS

SG   PF

PG   C   PF

SF

Although he spent almost his entire career playing for Chicago Bulls, Jordan retired three times in total: the first in 1993 after the death of his father, then, after rejoining the Bulls in 1995, he retired again in 1998, and he returned for a last hurrah with the Wizards from 2001 to 2003.

TOP 5 NOTABLE HONOURS
- 2x Olympic gold medal — Men's Basketball Team: (1984, 1992)
- 6x NBA champion: (1991–1993, 1996–1998)
- 6x NBA Finals MVP: (1991–1993, 1996–1998)
- 5x NBA Most Valuable Player: (1988, 1991, 1992, 1996, 1998)
- 3x NBA All-Star Game MVP: (1988, 1996, 1998)

DID YOU KNOW?
Jordan believed the shorts he wore to win his first National Championship were lucky. As a result, he wore his North Carolina practice shorts under his NBA uniform for good luck throughout his career.

NATIONALITY 🇺🇸 USA

2

TEAMS
San Antonio Spurs (2011-18),
Toronto Raptors (2018-19),
LA Clippers (2019–)

POSITION	Small Forward
ACTIVE YEARS	2011-present
DATE OF BIRTH	29 June 1991
BIRTHPLACE	Los Angeles, California
DRAFT	2011, R1 Pick 15
HEIGHT	200.7 cm (6 ft 7 in)

CAREER POINTS
13,725

APG
3.0

PPG
20.0

ALL-STAR GAMES
6

NBA MVP
0

ASSISTS
2,095

REBOUNDS
4,389

RPG
6.4

ACTIVE AREAS

SG

PF

PG

C

SF

KAWHI LEONARD

Kawhi Leonard — nicknamed 'The Klaw' — has earned a reputation as one of the NBA's greatest two-way players of all time. He also has an exceptional ability for ball-hawking (catching the ball or in stealing it from the opposing team).

Leonard made his name with the San Antonio Spurs, winning the first of his two NBA Championships there during a seven-year stay. He then moved to the Toronto Raptors for a year before joining LA Clippers. Athletic, strong, and hard-working, Leonard is regarded by many as a modern great.

TOP 5 NOTABLE HONOURS
- 2x NBA Champion: (2014, 2019)
- 2x NBA Finals MVP: (2014, 2019)
- NBA All-Star Game MVP: (2020)
- 3x All-NBA First Team: (2016, 2017, 2021)
- NBA 75th Anniversary Team

DID YOU KNOW?
Leonard, a huge fan of Hip-Hop, made a cameo appearance in Drake's music video for 'Way 2 Sexy'.

LISA LESLIE

The first player to dunk in WNBA history (2002), Lisa Leslie is a basketball legend who was an inspirational figure on and off the court. She spent her career with LA Sparks, where she became the first WNBA player to record 10,000 career PRA — a combination of points, rebounds and assists.

NATIONALITY 🇺🇸 USA

9

TEAMS
Los Angeles Sparks (1997-2009)

POSITION	Centre
ACTIVE YEARS	1997-2009
DATE OF BIRTH	7 July 1972
BIRTHPLACE	Compton California
DRAFT	1997 - Allocated*
HEIGHT	195.58 cm (6 ft 5 in)

CAREER POINTS
6,253

APG
25.1

PPG
17.3

ALL-STAR GAMES
8

WNBA MVP
3

ASSISTS
10,444

REBOUNDS
3,307

RPG
9.1

ACTIVE AREAS

SG
PF
PG
C
P
SF

Hailing out of the tough LA suburb of Compton, Leslie owes her opportunities to her mother, who started a truck-driving business to raise her three kids. It meant Leslie received a good college education, which carved a path for her into professional basketball and the inspiring legacy she created thereafter.

TOP 5 NOTABLE HONOURS
- 4x Olympic gold medal — Women's Basketball Team: (1996, 2000, 2004, 2008)
- 2x WNBA Champion: (2001, 2002)
- 2x WNBA Finals MVP: (2001, 2002)
- 8x All WNBA First Team: (1997, 200—04, 2006, 2008)
- 4x WNBA 10th, 15th, 20th, 25th Anniversary Team

DID YOU KNOW?
Leslie is a fashion model and an aspiring actress, as well as serving as a head coach for the Triplets — a 3v3 team in the BIG3 professional basketball league.

*As part of the 'Initial Allocation' phase of the draft when the WNBA was formed and started playing in 1997.

NATIONALITY 🇺🇸 USA

32 | 11

TEAMS
Utah Jazz (1985–2003),
LA Lakers (2003–04)

POSITION	Power Forward
ACTIVE YEARS	1985–2004
DATE OF BIRTH	24 July 1963
BIRTHPLACE	Summerfield, Louisiana
DRAFT	1985 R1 Pick 13
HEIGHT	205.7 cm (6 ft 9 in)

CAREER POINTS
36,928

APG
3.6

PPG
25.0

ALL-STAR GAMES
14

NBA MVP
2

ASSISTS
5,238

REBOUNDS
14,968

RPG
10.1

ACTIVE AREAS

SG

PF

PG

C

SF

KARL MALONE

Considered one of the greatest power forwards in NBA history, Malone's career points tally has been bettered only by the legendary LeBron James and Kareem Al-Jabbar. Malone spent 18 of his 19 career seasons with Utah Jazz where he is revered as their G.O.A.T.

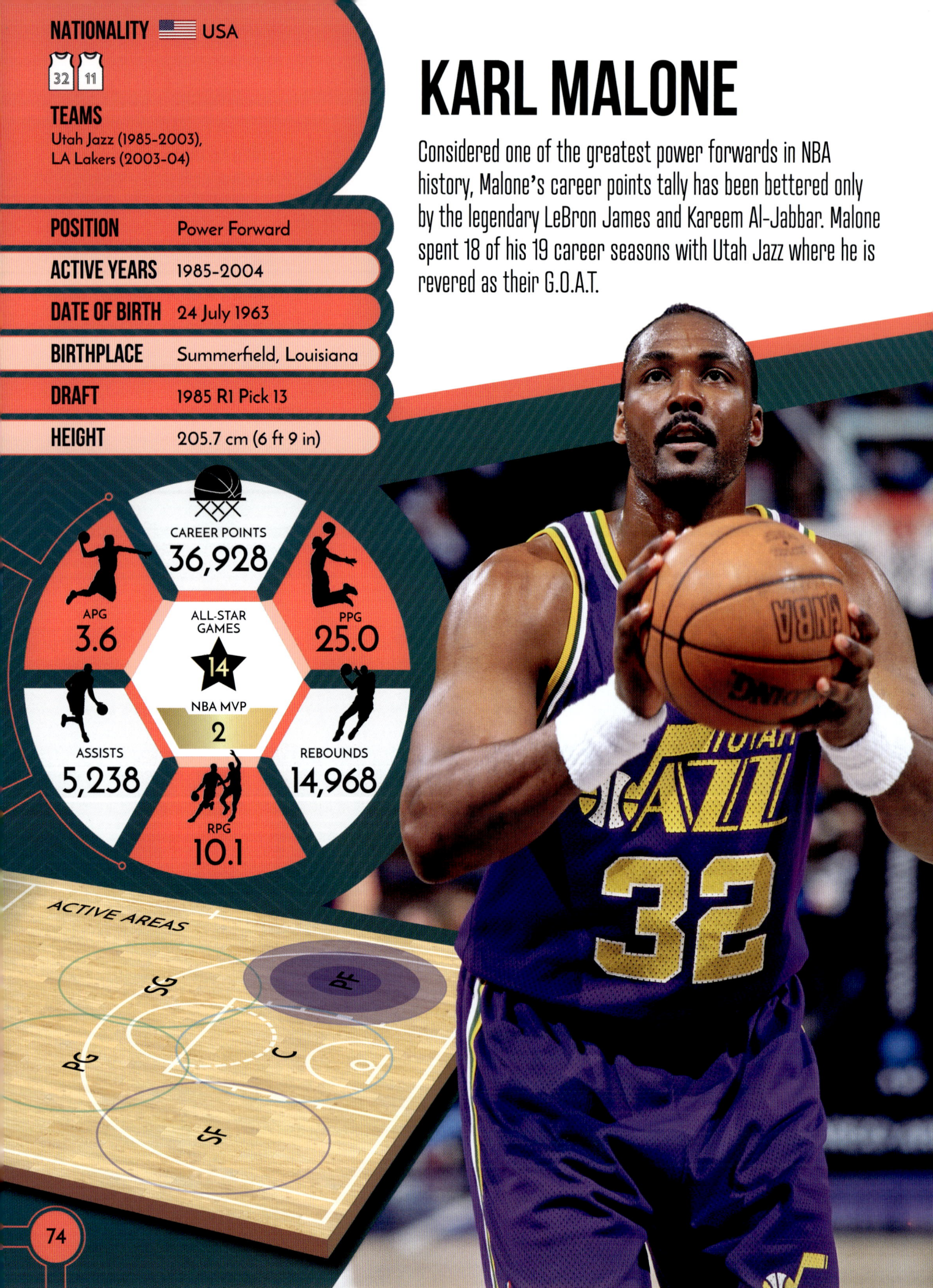

The only thing missing from Malone's wonderful career is an NBA champion's title — he spent the final year of his career with LA Lakers attempting to do just that — but he is a champion in every other sense of the word. Malone's nicknames 'The Mailman' and 'The Deliverer' bear testimony to a career defined by his prolific scoring.

TOP 5 NOTABLE HONOURS

- 2x Olympic gold medal — Men's Basketball Team: (1992, 1996)
- NBA 50th and 75th Anniversary Team
- All-Star Game MVP: (1989, 1993)
- 11x All-NBA First Team: (1989–1999)
- 2x All-NBA Second Team: (1988, 2000)

DID YOU KNOW?

In 1998, Malone wrestled Chicago Bulls power forward Dennis Rodman in a WCW professional match — Malone lost!

NATIONALITY 🇺🇸 USA

| 22 | 13 | 20 | 21 | 24 | 2 | 4 | 8 |

TEAMS Utah Stars (1974-75), Sp. of St. Louis (1975-76), Buff. Br. (1976), Houston Rockets (1976-82), Phil. 76ers (1982-86, '93-94), Wash. Bullets (1986-88), Atlanta Hawks (1988-91) Mil. Bucks (1991-93), San Antonio Spurs (1994-95)

POSITION	Centre
ACTIVE YEARS	1974-1995 (ABA & NBA)
DATE OF BIRTH	23 March 1955
BIRTHPLACE	Petersburg, Virginia
DRAFT	1974 Round 3
HEIGHT	208.3 cm (6 ft 10 in)

CAREER POINTS
29,580

APG **1.3**

PPG **20.3**

ALL-STAR GAMES **13**

NBA MVP **3**

ASSISTS **1,936**

REBOUNDS **17,834**

RPG **12.3**

ACTIVE AREAS

SG

PF

PG

C

SF

MOSES MALONE

Moses Malone's stellar career is capped by an NBA Championship win as well as a host of other top awards. Fast, strong and tenacious on the court, Malone grew into one of the best offensive rebounders ever seen, known for his shooting accuracy.

Most notably, Malone was the first player of the modern era to go into the professional circuit straight from high school and he lived up to that early promise.

He averaged 20 points or more per game for 11 consecutive seasons — a testimony to his talent, prowess and high level of consistency.

TOP 5 NOTABLE HONOURS
- 1x NBA Champion: (1983)
- 1 x NBA Finals MVP: (1983)
- NBA 50th and 75th Anniversary Team
- 6x NBA Rebounding Leader: (1979, 1981–85)
- Naismith Memorial Basketball Hall of Fame inductee: (2001)

DID YOU KNOW?
Even though Malone played in an aggressive style, he holds the NBA record for most consecutive games played without fouling out (1,212).

NATIONALITY 🇺🇸 USA

31

TEAMS
Indiana Pacers (1987-2005)

POSITION	Shooting Guard
ACTIVE YEARS	1987-2005
DATE OF BIRTH	24 August 1965
BIRTHPLACE	Riverside, California
DRAFT	1987 R1 Pick 11
HEIGHT	200.7 cm (6 ft 7 in)

REGGIE MILLER

Three-point shooting specialist Reggie Miller was ice cool under pressure and would shoot from distance with a focus and precision that made him among the best guards the sport has ever seen. He is one of the NBA's few major stars to spend his whole career with one team — Indiana Pacers in his case.

CAREER POINTS
25,279

APG
3.0

ALL-STAR GAMES
5

PPG
18.2

NBA MVP
0

ASSISTS
4,141

REBOUNDS
4,182

RPG
3.0

ACTIVE AREAS

SG

PF

PG

C

SF

78

Miller's speciality was his spectacular clutch shot, exemplified by the amazing play-off moments against the NY Knicks in 1994 and Chicago Bulls in 1998. He ended his career in 2005 with the highest number of three-pointers to his name, though that record has since been surpassed.

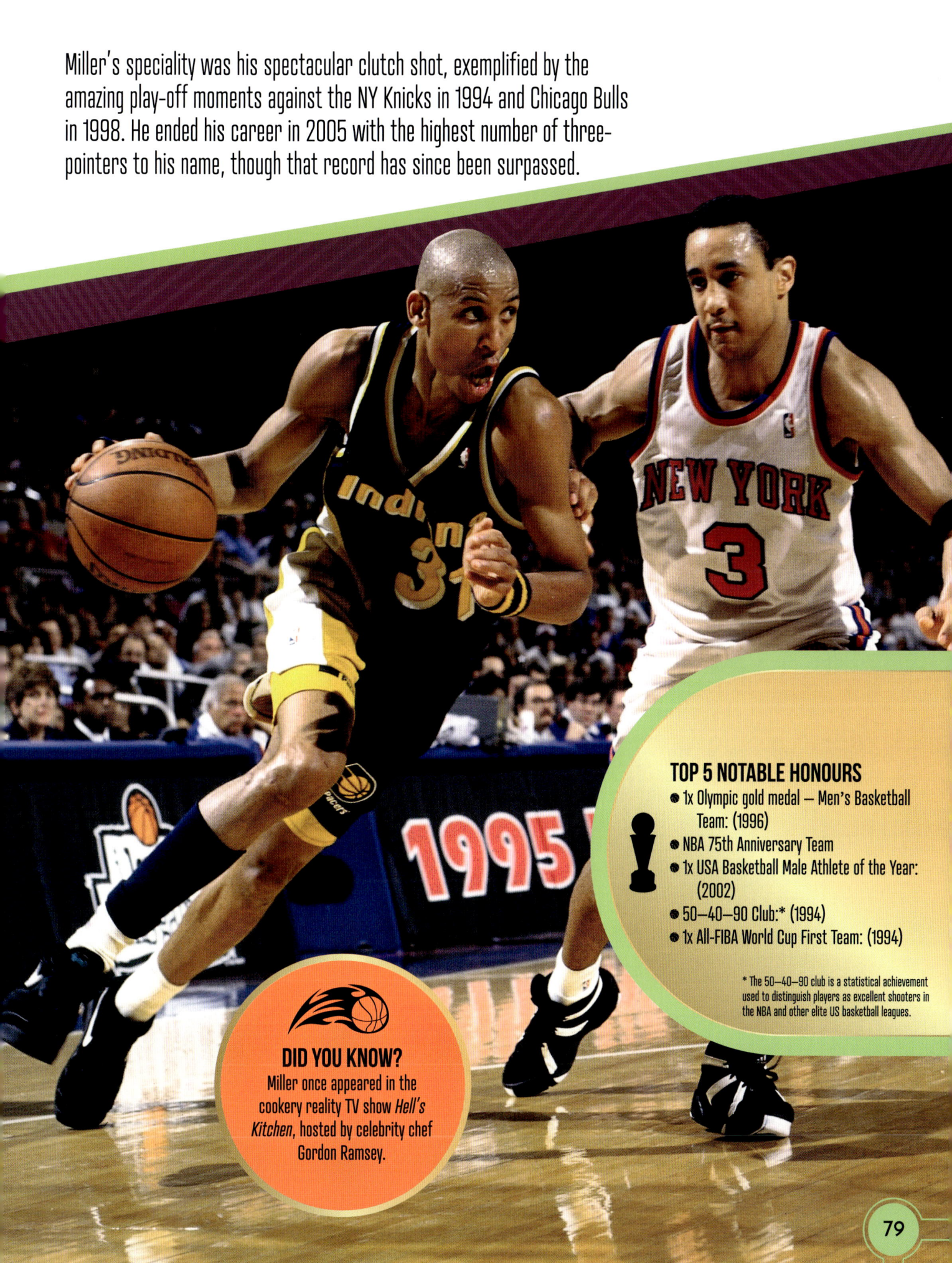

DID YOU KNOW?
Miller once appeared in the cookery reality TV show *Hell's Kitchen*, hosted by celebrity chef Gordon Ramsey.

TOP 5 NOTABLE HONOURS
- 1x Olympic gold medal — Men's Basketball Team: (1996)
- NBA 75th Anniversary Team
- 1x USA Basketball Male Athlete of the Year: (2002)
- 50–40–90 Club:* (1994)
- 1x All-FIBA World Cup First Team: (1994)

* The 50–40–90 club is a statistical achievement used to distinguish players as excellent shooters in the NBA and other elite US basketball leagues.

41

TEAMS
Dallas Mavericks (1994-2019)

DIRK NOWITZKI

One of the few Europeans to make the grade in the elite US league, Nowitzki is regarded not only as one of the greatest power forwards to grace the NBA, but perhaps the greatest basketball player Europe has ever produced.

POSITION	Pw. Forward/Centre
ACTIVE YEARS	1994-2019
DATE OF BIRTH	19 June 1978
BIRTHPLACE	Würzburg, Germany
DRAFT	1998 R1 Pick 9
HEIGHT	213.4 cm (7 ft)

CAREER POINTS
31,560

APG
2.4

PPG
20.7

ALL-STAR GAMES
14

NBA MVP
1

ASSISTS
3,651

REBOUNDS
11,489

RPG
7.5

ACTIVE AREAS

SG

PF

PG

C

SF

A versatile player with excellent shooting ability, his fadeaway jump shot became his trademark move, proving that big men were capable of being effective from long range. Nowitzki played his entire 21-year career with Dallas Mavericks, becoming an NBA legend in the process.

DID YOU KNOW?
Nowitzki's 21-year stay with the Mavericks is the longest any player has stayed with one team.

TOP 5 NOTABLE HONOURS
- 1x NBA Champion: (2011)
- 1x NBA Finals MVP: (2011)
- NBA 75th Anniversary Team
- 4x All-NBA First Team: (2005—2007, 2009)
- 1x NBA Three-Point Contest Champion: (2006)

NATIONALITY 🇺🇸 Nigeria/USA

34

TEAMS
Houston Rockets (1984-2001)
Toronto Raptors (2001-02)

POSITION	Centre
ACTIVE YEARS	1984-2002
DATE OF BIRTH	24 January 1963
BIRTHPLACE	Lagos, Nigeria
DRAFT	1984 R1 Pick 1
HEIGHT	213.4 cm (7 ft)

HAKEEM OLAJUWON

Nicknamed 'Hakeem the Dream', Olajuwon is considered one of NBA's all-time greatest centres. The No.1 pick of a draft that included Michael Jordan, Nigerian-born Olajuwon went on to spend 18 seasons with the Houston Rockets before joining the Toronto Raptors for the final year of his career.

CAREER POINTS
26,946

APG
2.5

PPG
21.8

ALL-STAR GAMES
12

NBA MVP
1

ASSISTS
3,058

REBOUNDS
13,747

RPG
11.1

ACTIVE AREAS

SG PF PG C SF

The only player in NBA history to record 200 steals and 200 blocks in a single season, he was excellent both as an offensive and defensive player. A terrific stealer of the ball, he was quick, possessed heavenly footwork and was a brilliant rebounder.

TOP 5 NOTABLE HONOURS
- 1x Olympic gold medal – Men's Basketball Team: (1996)
- 2x NBA Champion: (1994, 1995)
- 2x NBA Finals MVP: (1994, 1995)
- 6x All-NBA First Team: (1987–89, 1993, 1994, 1997)
- NBA 50th and 75th Anniversary Team

DID YOU KNOW?
Olajuwon refused to sign a big-money footwear deal, instead endorsing the budget-range brand Etonic Shoes — a brand poorer, working class parents could afford to buy their kids.

NATIONALITY 🇺🇸 USA

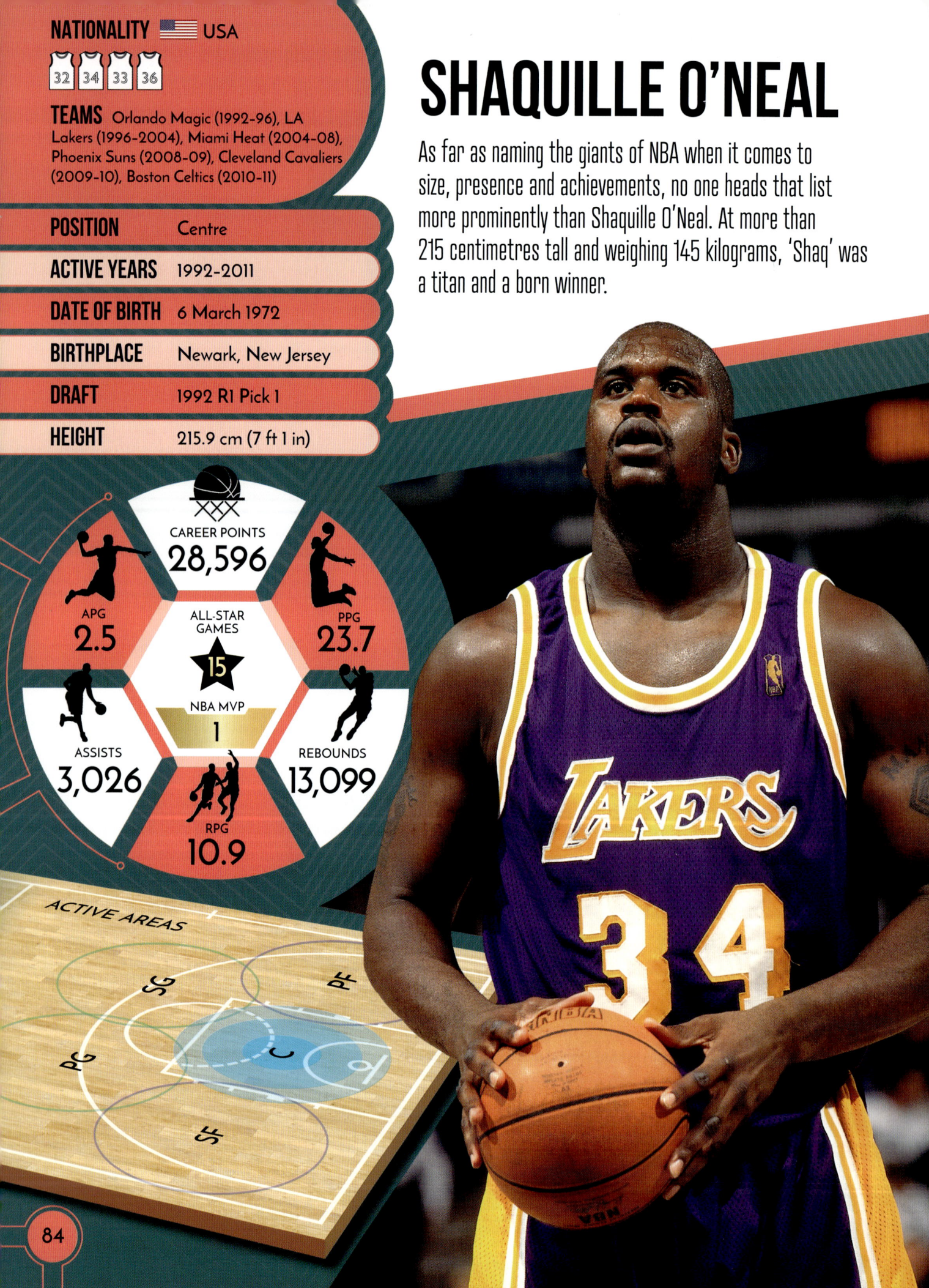

32 · 34 · 33 · 36

TEAMS Orlando Magic (1992-96), LA Lakers (1996-2004), Miami Heat (2004-08), Phoenix Suns (2008-09), Cleveland Cavaliers (2009-10), Boston Celtics (2010-11)

POSITION Centre

ACTIVE YEARS 1992-2011

DATE OF BIRTH 6 March 1972

BIRTHPLACE Newark, New Jersey

DRAFT 1992 R1 Pick 1

HEIGHT 215.9 cm (7 ft 1 in)

CAREER POINTS
28,596

APG 2.5

PPG 23.7

ALL-STAR GAMES 15

NBA MVP 1

ASSISTS 3,026

REBOUNDS 13,099

RPG 10.9

ACTIVE AREAS

SG · PF · PG · C · PF · SF

SHAQUILLE O'NEAL

As far as naming the giants of NBA when it comes to size, presence and achievements, no one heads that list more prominently than Shaquille O'Neal. At more than 215 centimetres tall and weighing 145 kilograms, 'Shaq' was a titan and a born winner.

84

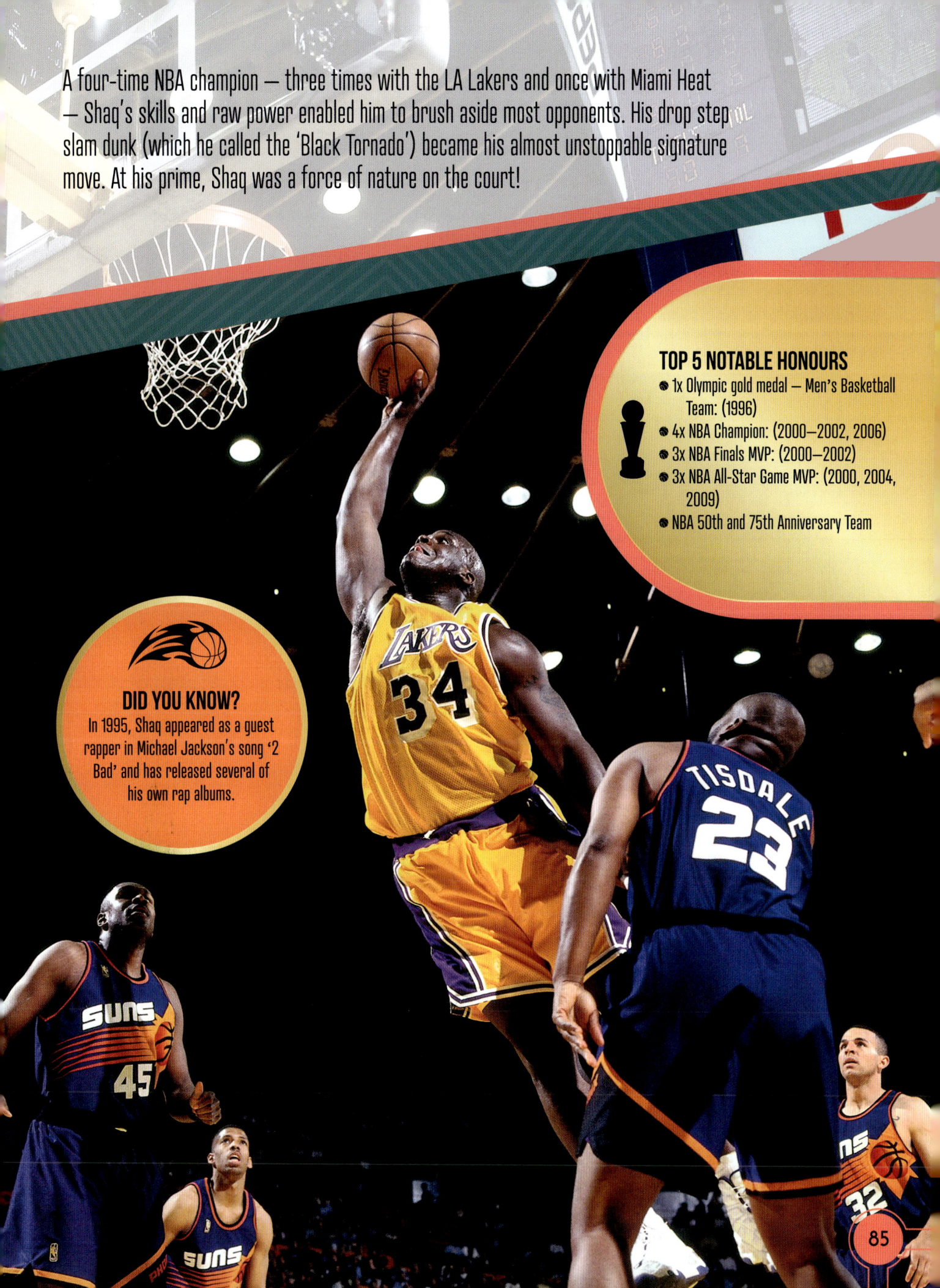

A four-time NBA champion — three times with the LA Lakers and once with Miami Heat — Shaq's skills and raw power enabled him to brush aside most opponents. His drop step slam dunk (which he called the 'Black Tornado') became his almost unstoppable signature move. At his prime, Shaq was a force of nature on the court!

TOP 5 NOTABLE HONOURS

- 1x Olympic gold medal — Men's Basketball Team: (1996)
- 4x NBA Champion: (2000–2002, 2006)
- 3x NBA Finals MVP: (2000–2002)
- 3x NBA All-Star Game MVP: (2000, 2004, 2009)
- NBA 50th and 75th Anniversary Team

DID YOU KNOW?

In 1995, Shaq appeared as a guest rapper in Michael Jackson's song '2 Bad' and has released several of his own rap albums.

3

TEAMS LA Sparks (2008-20), Chicago Sky (2021-22), **Las Vegas Aces (2023–)** *Abroad:* UMMC (2010-15), Guangdong Dolphins (2016), Fenerbahçe (2017), Xinjiang Tianshan Deers (2017-18)

POSITION	Power Forward
ACTIVE YEARS	2008-present
DATE OF BIRTH	19 April 1986
BIRTHPLACE	St Louis, Missouri
DRAFT	2008 R1 Pick 1
HEIGHT	193.04 cm (6 ft 4 in)

CANDACE PARKER

Regarded as one of the best female basketballers of all time, Candace Parker has been setting standards in the WNBA, especially during the 13 seasons she spent with LA Sparks. Nicknamed 'Ace', Parker's versatility and winning mentality on and off the court are her great strengths.

CAREER POINTS
6,574

APG
3.6

PPG
16.0

ALL-STAR GAMES
7

WNBA MVP
2

ASSISTS
1,634

REBOUNDS
3,467

RPG
8.5

ACTIVE AREAS

SG

PF

PG

C

SF

Such is Parker's professionalism that during each WNBA off-season from 2010 to 2015, she played for teams in Russia, Turkey and China, winning five championships in the Russian league. She even paused her career in 2009 to become a mother before returning to her glittering career.

TOP 5 NOTABLE HONOURS
- 2x Olympic gold medal – Women's Basketball Team: (2008, 2012)
- 3x WNBA Champion: (2016, 2021, 2023)
- 1x WNBA Finals MVP: (2016)
- 1x WNBA All-Star Game MVP: (2013)
- 7x All-WNBA First Team: (2008, 2012–14, 2017, 2020, 2022)

DID YOU KNOW?
In May 2007, People magazine listed Candace on their 100 World's Most Beautiful People list.

3

TEAMS New Orleans Hornets (2005–11), LA Clippers (2011–17), Houston Rockets (2017–19), Oklahoma City Thunder (2019–20), Phoenix Suns (2020–23), **Golden State Warriors (2023–)**

POSITION	Point Guard
ACTIVE YEARS	2005–present
DATE OF BIRTH	6 May 1985
BIRTHPLACE	Winston-Salem, North Carolina
DRAFT	2005 R1 Pick 4
HEIGHT	182.9 cm (6 ft)

CHRIS PAUL

Chris Paul, aka 'CP3' and 'The Point God', is regarded as one of the best point guards ever. Paul is dedicated to defence, but is also known for his court vision and fast thinking which have turned him into an assist king with more than 11,000 to his name so far.

CAREER POINTS
22,135

APG
9.4

PPG
17.6

ALL-STAR GAMES
12

NBA MVP
0

ASSISTS
11,790

REBOUNDS
5,616

RPG
4.5

ACTIVE AREAS

SG

PF

PG

C

SF

Standing at just 182 centimetres, he uses his superior agility to great effect at the back of the court. He is a key player for the Warriors and is highly respected within the sport.

TOP 5 NOTABLE HONOURS
- 2x Olympic gold medal — Men's Basketball Team: (2008, 2012)
- 1x NBA All-Star Game MVP: (2013)
- 4x All-NBA First Team: (2008, 2012—2014)
- NBA 75th Anniversary Team
- 7x NBA All-Defensive First Team: (2009, 2012—2017)

DID YOU KNOW?
In 2012, Chris Paul bought his Bel Air mansion from Canadian singer-songwriter Avril Lavigne. He sold the house in 2017.

NATIONALITY 🇺🇸 USA

33

TEAMS Chicago Bulls (1987-98, 2003-04), Houston Rockets (1999), Portland Trail Blazers (1999-2004), Torpan Pojat - *Finnish league* (2008), Sundsvall - *Swedish league* (2008)

POSITION	Small Forward
ACTIVE YEARS	1987-2004, 2008
DATE OF BIRTH	25 September 1965
BIRTHPLACE	Hamburg, Arkansas
DRAFT	1987 R1 Pick 5
HEIGHT	203.2 cm (6 ft 8 in)

SCOTTIE PIPPEN

One of the NBA's all-time greatest forwards, Scottie Pippen was a six-time NBA champion, a double Olympic gold medallist and a Chicago Bulls legend. Alongside Michael Jordan, Pippen helped the Bulls become a force and played his part in helping basketball become globally popular.

CAREER POINTS
18,940

APG
5.2

PPG
16.1

ALL-STAR GAMES
7

NBA MVP
0

ASSISTS
6,135

REBOUNDS
7,494

RPG
6.4

ACTIVE AREAS

SG

PF

PG

C

SF

His versatility was his strength, with an ability to excel in several different positions, making him what some call a 'multidimensional' player. A giant in defence too, his ability to block and steal led to him once being described as a 'one-man wrecking crew'.

TOP 5 NOTABLE HONOURS
- 2x Olympic gold medal — Men's Basketball Team: (1992, 1996)
- 6x NBA Champion: (1991, 1992, 1993, 1996, 1997, 1998)
- NBA All-Star Game MVP: (1994)
- 3x All-NBA First Team: (1994, 1995, 1996)
- NBA 50th and 75th Anniversary Team

DID YOU KNOW?
In April 2011, Chicago Bulls unveiled a bronze statue of Pippen outside their home arena — the United Center.

14 1

TEAMS
Cincinnati Royals (1960-70),
Milwaukee Bucks (1970-74)

POSITION	Point Guard
ACTIVE YEARS	1960-1974
DATE OF BIRTH	24 November 1938
BIRTHPLACE	Charlotte, Tennessee
DRAFT	1960 territorial pick
HEIGHT	195.6 cm (6 ft 5 in)

OSCAR ROBERTSON

Nicknamed 'The Big O', Oscar Robertson was the first player in NBA history to achieve a triple-double average over a season. This is when a player averages ten or more in a season in three different categories, which can be points, rebounds, steals, assists and blocked shots.

CAREER POINTS
26,710

APG
9.5

PPG
25.7

ALL-STAR GAMES
12

NBA MVP
1

ASSISTS
9,887

REBOUNDS
7,804

RPG
7.5

ACTIVE AREAS

SG

PF

PG

C

SF

92

Able to score from anywhere, Robertson had a silky-smooth playing style. He was incredibly nimble for his size, be it driving with the ball or finding a teammate with a quick pass, which made him a fantastic team player. His all-round skills made him a pioneer of the modern 'positionless' game.

TOP 5 NOTABLE HONOURS
- 1x Olympic gold medal – Men's Basketball Team: (1960)
- 1x NBA Champion: (1971)
- 3x NBA All-Star Game MVP: (1961, 1964, 1969)
- 9x All-NBA First Team: (1961–1969)
- NBA 35th, 50th and 75th Anniversary Team

DID YOU KNOW?
Between 1965 and 1974, Robertson served as the president of the NBA Players' Association. During his tenure, he led reforms that have since improved the lives and salaries of generations of players.

50

TEAMS
San Antonio Spurs (1989-2003)

POSITION	Centre
ACTIVE YEARS	1989-2003
DATE OF BIRTH	6 August 1965
BIRTHPLACE	Key West, Florida
DRAFT	1987 R1 Pick 1
HEIGHT	215.9 cm (7 ft 1 in)

DAVID ROBINSON

After serving in the US Navy, David Robinson entered the NBA as a polished 24-year-old. His athleticism made him explosively quick, which was combined with wonderful ball-handling skills and an offensive repertoire that would stay with him throughout his career. His mid-range jump shot was his signature move.

CAREER POINTS
20,790

APG
2.5

PPG
21.1

ALL-STAR GAMES
10

NBA MVP
1

ASSISTS
2,954

REBOUNDS
10,497

RPG
10.6

ACTIVE AREAS

SG

PF

PG

SF

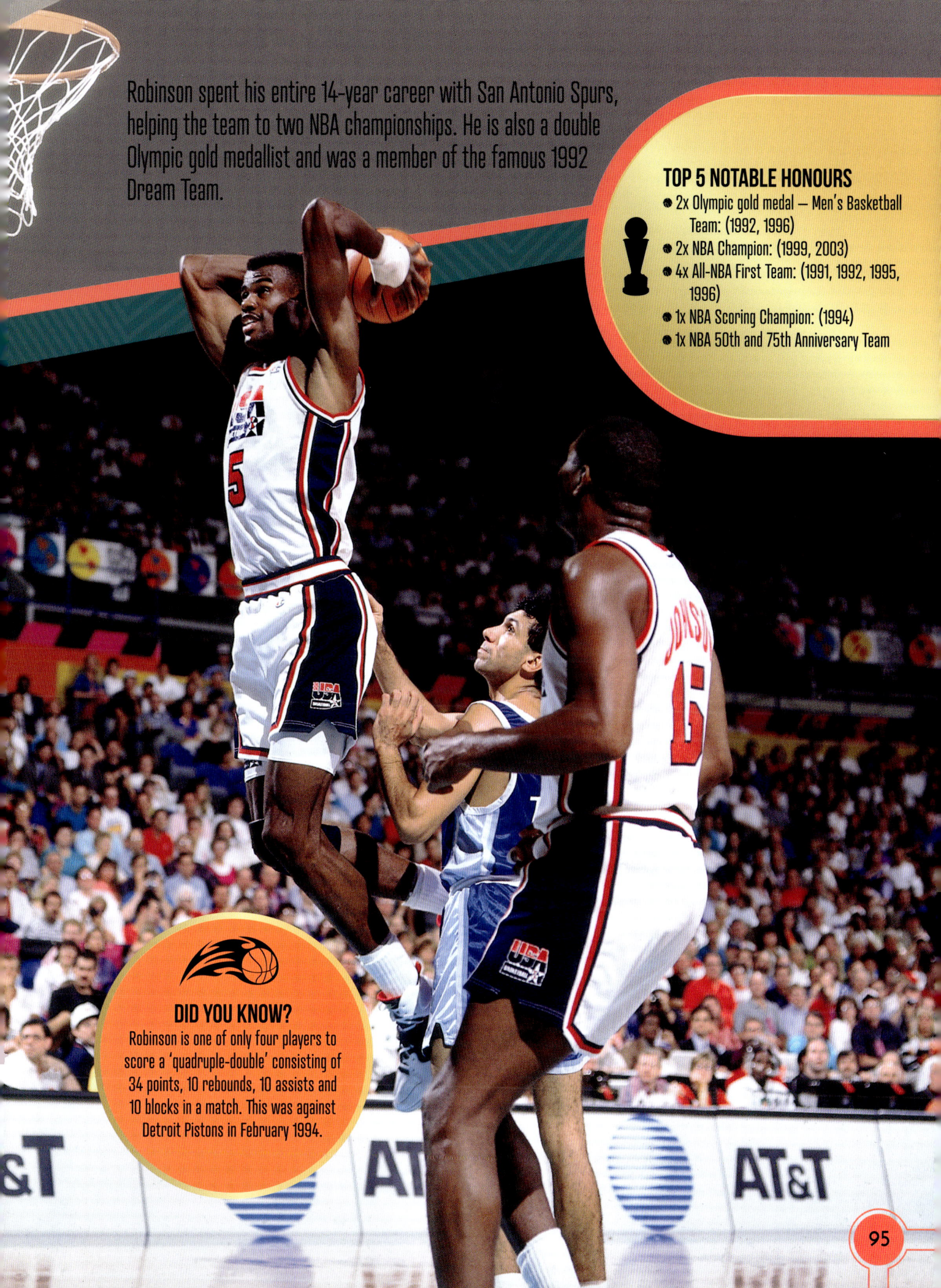

Robinson spent his entire 14-year career with San Antonio Spurs, helping the team to two NBA championships. He is also a double Olympic gold medallist and was a member of the famous 1992 Dream Team.

TOP 5 NOTABLE HONOURS
- 2x Olympic gold medal — Men's Basketball Team: (1992, 1996)
- 2x NBA Champion: (1999, 2003)
- 4x All-NBA First Team: (1991, 1992, 1995, 1996)
- 1x NBA Scoring Champion: (1994)
- 1x NBA 50th and 75th Anniversary Team

DID YOU KNOW?
Robinson is one of only four players to score a 'quadruple-double' consisting of 34 points, 10 rebounds, 10 assists and 10 blocks in a match. This was against Detroit Pistons in February 1994.

NATIONALITY 🇺🇸 USA

| 10 | 91 | 73 | 70 |

TEAMS Detroit Pistons (1986-93), San Antonio Spurs (1993-95), Chicago Bulls (1995-98), LA Lakers 1999, Dallas Mavericks (2000), Long Beach Jam (2003-04)

POSITION	Pw. Forward/Sm. Forward
ACTIVE YEARS	1986-2006
DATE OF BIRTH	13 May 1961
BIRTHPLACE	Trenton, New Jersey
DRAFT	1996 R2 Pick 27
HEIGHT	200.7 cm (6 ft 7 in)

CAREER POINTS
6,683

APG
1.8

PPG
7.3

ALL-STAR GAMES
2

NBA MVP
0

ASSISTS
1,600

REBOUNDS
11,954

RPG
13.1

ACTIVE AREAS

SG

PF

PG

C

SF

DENNIS RODMAN

Fierce in defence and one of the best players at rebounding in NBA history, Dennis Rodman was as colourful and controversial as he was successful. As a five-time NBA champion, he more than proved his worth, developing from a small forward to a power forward with equal success.

A hustler on the court, he would often clash with opponents and officials, making life with Rodman on court rarely dull. Like many players, Rodman had his weaknesses, but in areas he excelled he was a world-beater.

TOP 5 NOTABLE HONOURS
- 5x NBA Champion: (1989, 1990, 1996, 1997, 1998)
- NBA 75th Anniversary Team
- 7x NBA Rebounding Champion: (1992—1998)
- 7x NBA All-Defensive First Team: (1989—1993, 1995, 1996)
- 1x NBA All-Defensive Second Team: (1994)

DID YOU KNOW?
Of Dennis Rodman's many adventures outside basketball, he was a professional wrestler and a reality TV star!

NATIONALITY 🇺🇸 USA

Number 6

TEAMS
Boston Celtics (1956-69)

POSITION	Centre
ACTIVE YEARS	1956-1969
DATE OF BIRTH	12 February 1934
BIRTHPLACE	Monroe, Louisiana
DRAFT	1956 R1 Pick 2
HEIGHT	208.3 cm (6 ft 10 in)

BILL RUSSELL

The legendary Bill Russell was an immense talent who helped Boston Celtics to an astonishing 11 NBA Championships. He was brilliant at playing man-to-man defence, blocking shots, and grabbing defensive and offensive rebounds.

CAREER POINTS
14,522

ALL-STAR GAMES
12

NBA MVP
5

APG
4.3

PPG
15.1

ASSISTS
4,100

REBOUNDS
21,620

RPG
22.5

ACTIVE AREAS

SG · PF · PG · C · SF

A rebound phenomenon, he became the first player in NBA history to average 20+ rebounds per game. In fact, he achieved this in 10 out of the 13 seasons he played in the NBA. He is only second to his close friend Wilt Chamberlain in the most number of rebound points scored in NBA history.

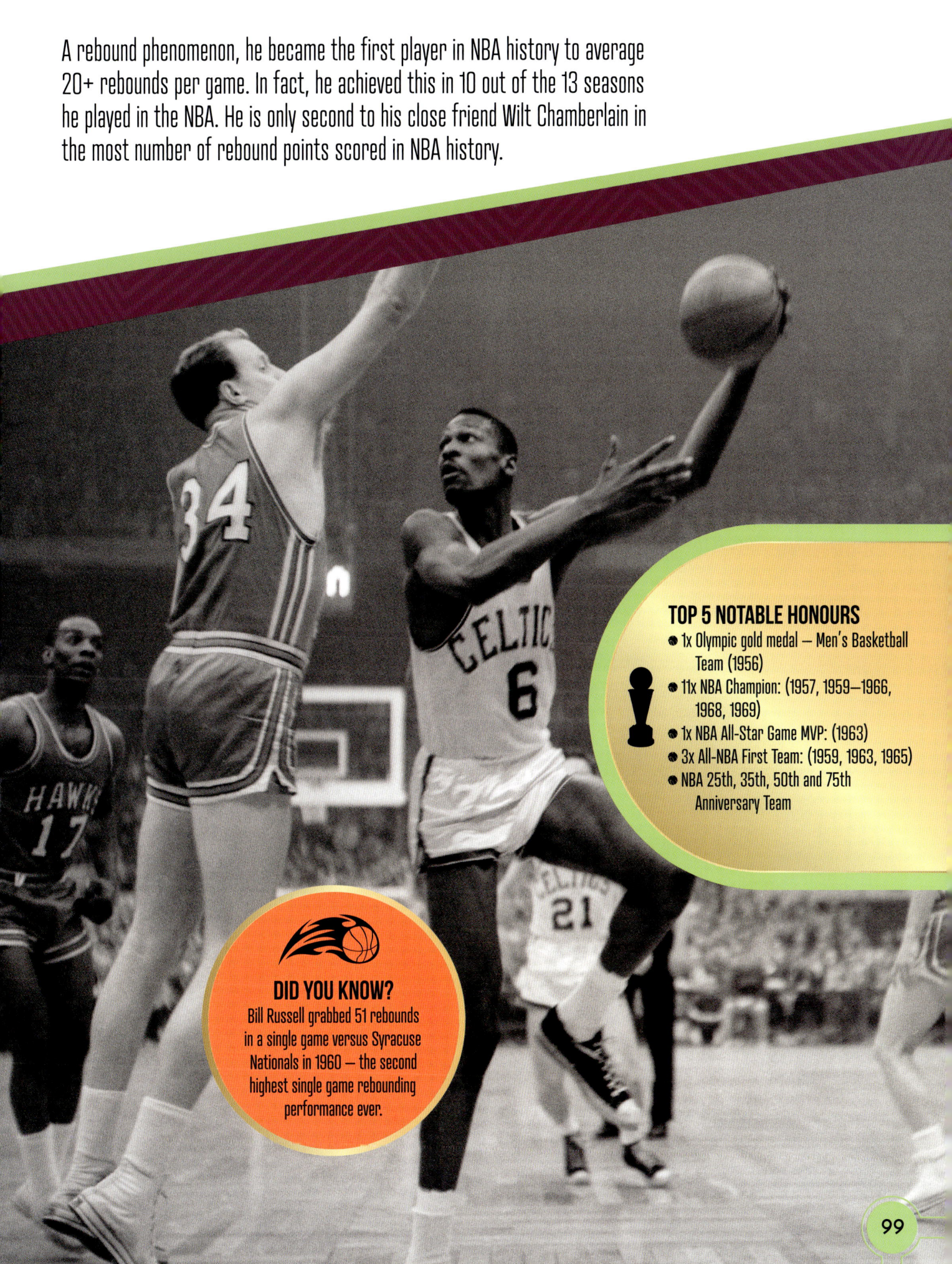

TOP 5 NOTABLE HONOURS
- 1x Olympic gold medal – Men's Basketball Team (1956)
- 11x NBA Champion: (1957, 1959–1966, 1968, 1969)
- 1x NBA All-Star Game MVP: (1963)
- 3x All-NBA First Team: (1959, 1963, 1965)
- NBA 25th, 35th, 50th and 75th Anniversary Team

DID YOU KNOW?
Bill Russell grabbed 51 rebounds in a single game versus Syracuse Nationals in 1960 – the second highest single game rebounding performance ever.

NATIONALITY 🇺🇸 USA

12

TEAMS
Utah Jazz

POSITION	Point Guard
ACTIVE YEARS	1984-2003
DATE OF BIRTH	26 March 1962
BIRTHPLACE	Spokane, Washington
DRAFT	1984 R1 Pick 16
HEIGHT	185.4 cm (6 ft 1 in)

JOHN STOCKTON

A brilliant point guard and superb passer, John Stockton spent his entire 19-year career with Utah Jazz — and helped the team make the play-offs in all of his 19 seasons. A tireless worker for the team, he holds the NBA records for the most steals and assists by a wide margin.

CAREER POINTS
19,711

APG
10.5

PPG
13.1

ALL-STAR GAMES
10

NBA MVP
0

ASSISTS
15,806

REBOUNDS
4,051

RPG
2.7

ACTIVE AREAS

SG

PF

PG

C

SF

He was regarded as one of the toughest players of his generation, happy to do the dirty work and let others take the limelight in front of the hoop. Consistency and longevity are also two defining features of Stockton's career.

TOP 5 NOTABLE HONOURS
- 2x Olympic gold medal – Men's Basketball Team: (1992, 1996)
- 1x NBA All-Star Game MVP: (1993)
- 2x All-NBA First Team: (1994, 1995)
- 9x NBA Assists Leader: (1988–1996)
- NBA 50th and 75th Anniversary Team

DID YOU KNOW?
John Stockton preferred shorter shorts rather than the standard longer ones – these became known as 'Stocktons'.

NATIONALITY 🇺🇸 USA

3

TEAMS Phoenix Mercury (2004–)
Abroad: Dynamo Moscow (2005-06), Spartak Moscow (2006-10), Fenerbahçe (2010-11), Galatasaray S.K. (2011-12), UMMC (2012-17).

POSITION	Po. Guard/Sh. Guard
ACTIVE YEARS	2004-present
DATE OF BIRTH	11 June 1982
BIRTHPLACE	Chino, California
DRAFT	2004 R1 Pick 1
HEIGHT	182.88 cm (6 ft)

DIANA TAURASI

Another WNBA legend, Diana Taurasi has spent 20 seasons at the top and is known for her shooting, playmaking skills and clutch moments. She is one of only a few athletes to win five gold medals at five different Olympic Games.

CAREER POINTS
10,108

APG
4.3

PPG
19.1

ALL-STAR GAMES
10

WNBA MVP
1

ASSISTS
1,851

REBOUNDS
1,164

RPG
3.9

ACTIVE AREAS

SG

PF

PG

C

SF

In 2011, fans voted her in the top 15 all-time greatest players and 10 years later, she was voted the greatest of all time! Taurasi has plied her trade abroad too, winning multiple titles in the European, Russian and Turkish leagues. Back home, she became the first WNBA player to score 10,000+ points in 2023 and continues to break records and create history.

DID YOU KNOW?
NBA legend Kobe Bryant gave Taurasi the nickname 'White Mamba' because of her aggressive playing style and scoring ability.

TOP 5 NOTABLE HONOURS
- 5x Olympic gold medal – Women's Basketball Team (2004, 2008, 2012, 2016, 2020)
- 3x WNBA Champion: (2007, 2009, 2014)
- 2x WNBA Finals MVP: (2009, 2014)
- 10x All-WNBA First Team (2004, 2006-11, 2013-14, 2018)
- NBA 15th, 20th and 25th Anniversary Team

11

TEAMS
Detroit Pistons

POSITION	Point Guard
ACTIVE YEARS	1981–1994
DATE OF BIRTH	30 April 1961
BIRTHPLACE	Chicago, Illinois
DRAFT	1981 R1 Pick 2
HEIGHT	185.4 cm (6 ft 1 in)

ISIAH THOMAS

When Michael Jordan rates you as the second greatest point guard of all-time (behind Magic Johnson), you know you have left a legacy in the sport! Isiah Thomas spent his entire NBA career with Detroit Pistons, where his skills in defence contributed hugely to the team's success.

CAREER POINTS
18,622

APG
9.3

ALL-STAR GAMES
⭐ **12**

PPG
19.2

NBA MVP
0

ASSISTS
9,061

REBOUNDS
3,478

RPG
3.6

ACTIVE AREAS

SG · PF · PG · C · SF

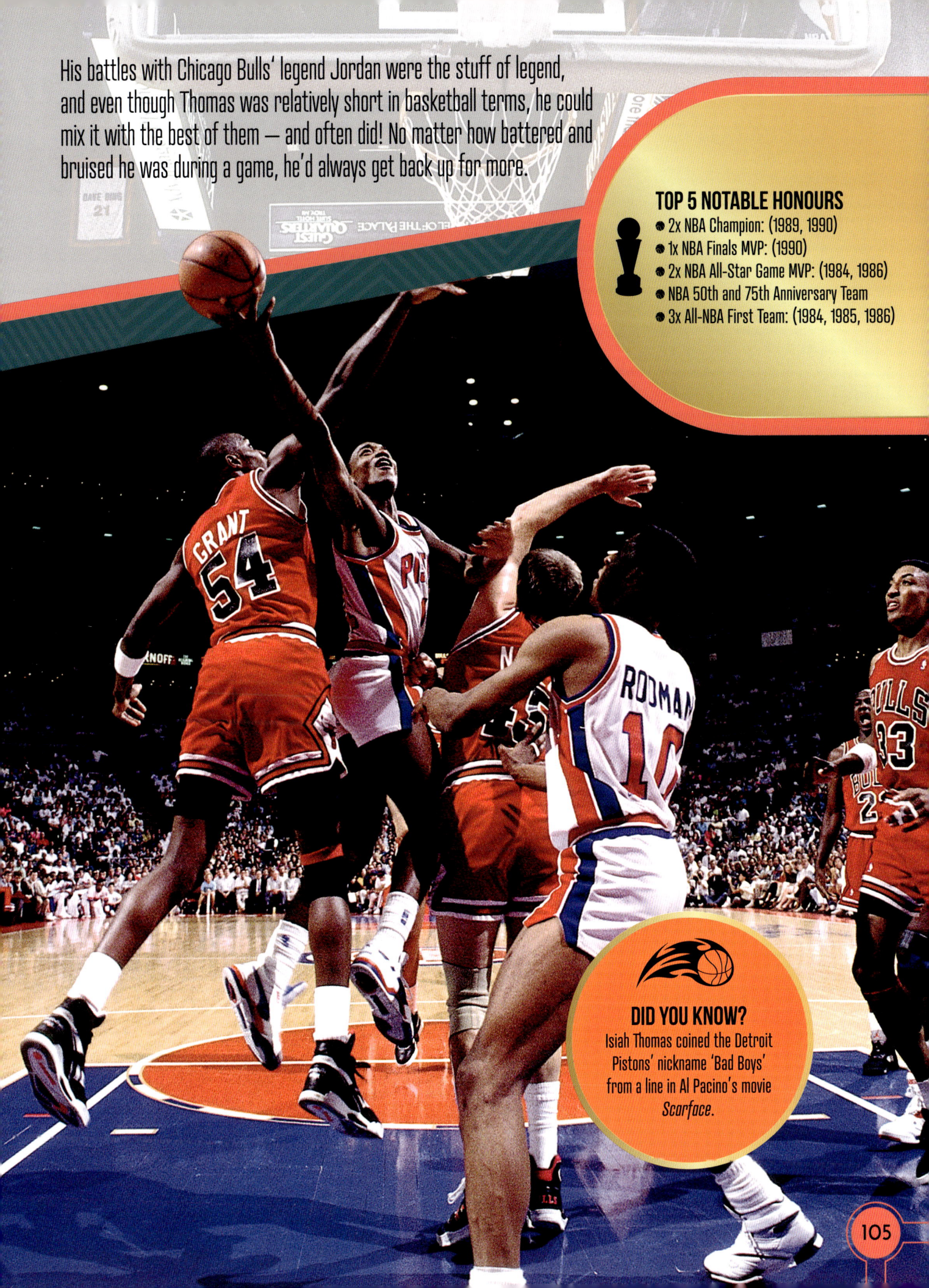

His battles with Chicago Bulls' legend Jordan were the stuff of legend, and even though Thomas was relatively short in basketball terms, he could mix it with the best of them — and often did! No matter how battered and bruised he was during a game, he'd always get back up for more.

TOP 5 NOTABLE HONOURS
- 2x NBA Champion: (1989, 1990)
- 1x NBA Finals MVP: (1990)
- 2x NBA All-Star Game MVP: (1984, 1986)
- NBA 50th and 75th Anniversary Team
- 3x All-NBA First Team: (1984, 1985, 1986)

DID YOU KNOW?
Isiah Thomas coined the Detroit Pistons' nickname 'Bad Boys' from a line in Al Pacino's movie *Scarface*.

NATIONALITY 🇺🇸 USA

| 3 | 9 |

TEAMS
Miami Heat (2003-16, 2018-19),
Chicago Bulls (2016-17),
Cleveland Cavaliers (2017-18)

POSITION	Sh. Guard/Po. Guard
ACTIVE YEARS	2003-2019
DATE OF BIRTH	17 January 1982
BIRTHPLACE	Chicago, Illinois
DRAFT	2003 R1 Pick 5
HEIGHT	193.0 cm (6 ft 4 in)

DWYANE WADE

Dwyane Wade could drive to the basket with incredible power and speed, which made him one of the best slashers ever. There were so many awesome aspects to Wade's offensive game, including his turnaround jump shot.

CAREER POINTS
23,165

APG
5.4

PPG
22.0

ALL-STAR GAMES
13

NBA MVP
0

ASSISTS
5,701

REBOUNDS
4,933

RPG
4.7

ACTIVE AREAS

SG

PF

PG

C

SF

An industrious and intelligent player, Wade was fearless in everything he did; even the risk of injury from mid-air collisions with bigger, more powerful opponents did little to stop him from his all-out approach.

DID YOU KNOW?
In 2006, Dwyane Wade was named the NBA's best dressed player by *GQ* magazine.

TOP 5 NOTABLE HONOURS
- 1x Olympic gold medal – Men's Basketball Team: (2008)
- 3x NBA Champion: (2006, 2012, 2013)
- 1x NBA Finals MVP: (2006)
- 1x NBA All-Star Game MVP: (2010)
- NBA 75th Anniversary Team

44

TEAMS
LA Lakers (1960-1974)

JERRY WEST

An LA Lakers player for his whole career, Jerry West was a guard who was equally adept at playmaking as he was at shooting. He was famed for his lightning quick jump shots while his speciality of scoring late baskets earned him the nickname 'Mr Clutch'.

POSITION	Po. Guard/Sh. Guard
ACTIVE YEARS	1960-1974
DATE OF BIRTH	28 May 1938
BIRTHPLACE	Cheylan, West Virginia
DRAFT	1960 R1 Pick 2
HEIGHT	190.5 cm (6 ft 3 in)

CAREER POINTS
25,192

APG
6.7

PPG
27.0

ALL-STAR GAMES
14

NBA MVP
0

ASSISTS
6,238

REBOUNDS
5,366

RPG
5.8

ACTIVE AREAS

SG

PF

PG

C

P

SF

Few players before or since can match his scoring average per game of 27 points, A cool, calm and focused player, West was a natural leader and integral to the Lakers' success in that era.

DID YOU KNOW?
The official NBA logo is composed of the silhouette of Jerry West.

NATIONALITY 🇺🇸 USA

4 | 0

TEAMS Oklahoma City Thunder (2008-19), Houston Rockets (2019-20), Washington Wizards (2020-21), LA Lakers (2021-23), **LA Clippers (2023—)**

POSITION	Point Guard
ACTIVE YEARS	2008-present
DATE OF BIRTH	12 November 1988
BIRTHPLACE	Long Beach, California
DRAFT	2008 R1 Pick 4
HEIGHT	193.0 cm (6 ft 4 in)

RUSSELL WESTBROOK

Russell Westbrook is a dominating figure on the court with phenomenal levels of stamina. He is also a highly productive playmaker, able to make a telling pass — averaging more than eight assists per game — or pull up for a mid-range jump shot.

CAREER POINTS
25,098

APG
8.2

ALL-STAR GAMES
9

PPG
21.8

NBA MVP
1

ASSISTS
9,418

REBOUNDS
8,258

RPG
7.2

ACTIVE AREAS

SG

PF

PG

C

SF

P

There are few point guards who can match Westbrook when it comes to his physical attributes. Currently, Westbrook's 198 season triple-doubles are the most in NBA history.

TOP 5 NOTABLE HONOURS

- 1x Olympic gold medal — Men's Basketball Team: (2012)
- 2x NBA All-Star Game MVP: (2015, 2016)
- 2x All-NBA First Team: (2016, 2017)
- 2x NBA Scoring Champion: (2015, 2017)
- NBA 75th Anniversary Team

DID YOU KNOW?

Russell Westbrook is passionate about fashion. Back in 2017, he even launched his own fashion brand called *Honor The Gift*.

FUTURE LEGENDS

Basketball icons such as Larry Bird, Michael Johnson and LeBron James may have set a high bar in the sport, but it is these standards that drive the current generation. Can these promising talents become the game's future legends?

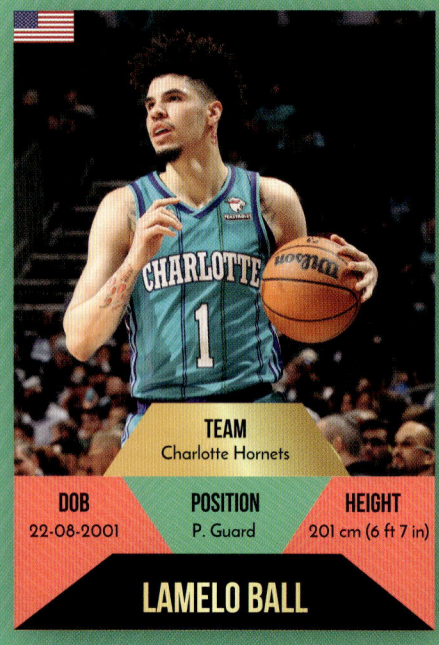

	TEAM	
	Charlotte Hornets	
DOB	**POSITION**	**HEIGHT**
22-08-2001	P. Guard	201 cm (6 ft 7 in)

LAMELO BALL

	TEAM	
	Indiana Fever	
DOB	**POSITION**	**HEIGHT**
11-12-2001	Pw F/Centre	196 cm (6 ft 5 in)

ALIYAH BOSTON

	TEAM	
	Iowa (Big Ten Conf.)	
BIRTHDATE	**POSITION**	**HEIGHT**
01-22-2002	Point Guard	6 ft. (183 cm)

CAITLIN CLARK

	TEAM	
	Oklahoma City Thunder	
DOB	**POSITION**	**HEIGHT**
1-05-2002	Centre/Pw F	215.9 cm (7 ft 1 in)

CHET HOLMGREN

	TEAM	
	Atlanta Dream	
DOB	**POSITION**	**HEIGHT**
29-04-2000	Sh. Guard	188 cm (6 ft 2 in)

RHYNE HOWARD

	TEAM	
	San Antonio Spurs	
DOB	**POSITION**	**HEIGHT**
4-01-2004	Pw F/Centre	224 cm (7 ft 4 in)

VICTOR WEMBANYAMA